ETHICS CASE BOOK

OF THE
AMERICAN PSYCHOANALYTIC
ASSOCIATION

EDITED BY
PAUL A. DEWALD, M.D.
AND RITA W. CLARK, M.D.

Associate Editors
Subcommittee on Ethics Revision

APsaA
AMERICAN PSYCHOANALYTIC ASSOCIATION
309 East 49th Street
New York, NY 10017-1601

SUBCOMMITTEE ON ETHICS REVISION

Marvin Margolis, M.D., Ph.D., Chair
Katherine A. Brunkow, M.S.W.
Murray T. Charlson, M.D.
Glen O. Gabbard, M.D.
Dorothy E. Holmes, Ph.D.
Irving L. Humphrey, III., M.D.
Jacob G. Jacobson, M.D.
Margaret C. Keenan, M.D.
Paulina F. Kernberg, M.D.
Katherine Macvicar, M.D.
Malkah T. Notman, M.D.
Cynthia Rose, M.D.
Bernard Rubin, M.D.
Evangeline J. Spindler, M.D.
Ernest Wallwork, Ph.D.

Grateful acknowledgment is made to
Frenkel & Company for its generous support of the
publication of the Ethics Case Book.

American Psychoanalytic Association
309 East 49th Street • New York, NY 10017-1601
Phone: 212-752-0450 • Email: info@apsa.org •
http://www.apsa.org/

ETHICS CASE BOOK

OF THE
AMERICAN PSYCHOANALYTIC
ASSOCIATION

*THE PRINCIPLES AND STANDARDS OF ETHICS FOR
PSYCHOANALYSIS ("PRINCIPLES") OF THE AMERICAN
PSYCHOANALYTIC ASSOCIATION EVOLVE OVER TIME TO
REFLECT ONGOING RESEARCH AND STUDY IN THE FIELD
AND THE IDENTIFICATION OF NEW AREAS OF CONCERN
FOR MEMBERS AND THEIR PATIENTS. THE VERSION OF THE
PRINCIPLES IN THE FRONT OF THIS CASEBOOK WAS
CURRENT AS OF 2007. FOR THE CURRENT VERSION OF
THE PRINCIPLES, PLEASE VISIT
http://www.apsa.org/*

CONTENTS

FOREWORD

*These revised Principles and Provisions were approved by the Executive Council and the Board on Professional Standards of The American Psychoanalytic Association in December 2000.

B. CONFIDENTIALITY

C. AVOIDING EXPLOITATION

D. RELATIONSHIPS WITH COLLEAGUES, STUDENTS, AND SUPERVISEES

E. SAFEGUARDING THE PUBLIC AND THE PROFESSION

FOREWORD

The Ethics Case Book was introduced six years ago to accompany the newly revised Ethics Code. It was thought that the code itself could not cover all of the complexities of actual practice where situations often involved conflicting provisions and the need to establish priorities. Following the code would also bring up personal conflicts and differing values. In other words, the code alone is not enough guidance in many situations.

The vignettes developed for the Case Book were intended to introduce the element of "real life situations" and to stimulate discussion and promote a balanced understanding of ethical principles and the many difficult choices that come up in practice. It was hoped that through discussion of the hypothetical issues the appreciation of ethical dilemmas would be enhanced and result in a more informed decision making process when actual problems occurred. It was also hoped that this would be a lively and personally meaningful vehicle for the teaching of ethics.

The response has been very positive and the Case Book is now used in many ethics courses in programs both within and outside of the American Psychoanalytic Association. It has been a useful tool for bringing ethics to the attention of analysts at all levels. Greater awareness results in more thoughtful attention to everyday situations that are problematic but might have been ignored in the past.

This second edition provides a more sophisticated and expanded group of vignettes and also allows for the correction of some of the errors and typos in the previous version.

Rita W. Clark, M.D.
Paul A. DeWald, M.D.

April 18, 2007

I.A

PRINCIPLES AND STANDARDS OF ETHICS FOR PSYCHOANALYSTS

Preamble:

Psychoanalysis is a method of treating children, adolescents and adults with emotional and mental disorders that attempts to reduce suffering and disability and enhance growth and autonomy. While the psychoanalytic relationship is predicated on respecting human dignity, it necessarily involves a power differential between psychoanalyst, patient and, particularly in the case of children, the family that, if ignored, trivialized or misused, can compromise or derail treatment and inflict significant damage on all parties*. Constant self examination and reflection by the psychoanalyst and liberal use of formal consultation are obvious safeguards for the patient, as well as for the treating psychoanalyst.

No code of ethics can be encyclopedic in providing answers to all ethical questions that may arise in the practice of

---

*When the patient is a child or adolescent (a minor) the parent(s) or guardian(s) play a significant role in the treatment. In these situations the functions of such a role changes with age, stage of development, diagnosis, as well as growth of capacity within the patient. How the psychoanalyst relates to the patient and family will reflect such changes. These shifts need to be dealt with in direct and open ways with all concerned. The potential power differential and transference-countertransference between psychoanalyst, patient and parenting figures (or other important family members) can be significant. If not recognized or mishandled such issues can interfere with the treatment and disrupt it.

i

the profession of psychoanalysis. Sound judgment and integrity of character are indispensable in applying ethical principles to particular situations and individuals. The major goal of this code is to facilitate the psychoanalyst's best efforts in all areas of analytic work and to encourage early and full discussion of ethical questions with colleagues and members of local and national ethics committees. These revised Principles presuppose a psychoanalyst's life-long commitment to act ethically and to encourage similar ethical behavior in colleagues and students. It is expected that over time all psychoanalysts will enrich and add cumulatively to the guidance provided by the Principles with their own experience and values, and that the Principles will evolve, based on the profession's insights and experience.

GENERAL PRINCIPLES OF ETHICS
FOR PSYCOANALYSTS

Introduction:

The American Psychoanalytic Association has adopted the following Principles of Ethics and associated Standards to guide members in their professional conduct toward their patients and, in the case of minors, toward their parent(s) or guardian(s) as well as supervisees, students, colleagues and the public. These Principles and Standards substantially revise and update the ethical principles contained in the previous Principles of Ethics published by the American Psychoanalytic Association in December 1975, and revised in 1983. The revisions take account of evolving moral sensibilities and observed deficiencies in the earlier codes. As ethical standards change, behaviors that were acceptable in the past may no longer be considered ethical. In this regard, however, these evolving standards should not be used to punish individuals retroactively. These revised principles emphasize constraints on behaviors that are likely to misuse the power differential of the transference-countertransference relationship to the detriment of patients and, in the case of minors, their parent (s) or guardian (s) as well.

The new code seeks to identify the parameters of the high standard of care expected of psychoanalysts in treatment, teaching, and research. By specifying standards of expected conduct, the code is intended to inform all psychoanalysts in considering and arriving at ethical courses of action and to alert members and candidates to departures from the wide range of acceptable practices. When doubts about the ethics of a psychoanalyst's conduct arise early intervention is encouraged. Experience indicates that when ethical violations are thought to have occurred, prompt consultation and mediation tend to serve the best interests of all parties concerned. When indicated, procedures for filing, investigating and resolving complaints of unethical conduct are addressed in the Provisions for Implementation of the Principles and Standards of Ethics for Psychoanalysts.

There are times when ethical principles conflict, making a choice of action difficult. In ordering ethical obligations, one's duty is to the patient directly, or indirectly through supervision or consultation with the treating psychoanalyst. In the case of patients who are minors there are also ethical obligations to parent(s) or guardian(s) which change as the patient becomes older and more mature. Thereafter, ethical obligations are to the profession, to students and colleagues, and to society. The ethical practice of psychoanalysis requires the psychoanalyst to be familiar with these Principles and Standards; to conduct regular self-examination; to seek consultation promptly when ethical questions arise; and to reach just sanctions when judging the actions of a colleague.

GUIDING GENERAL PRINCIPLES

I. Professional Competence. The psychoanalyst is committed to provide competent professional service. The psychoanalyst should continually strive to improve his or her knowledge and practical skills. Illnesses and personal problems that significantly impair the psychoanalyst's performance of professional responsibilities should be acknowledged and addressed in appropriate fashion as soon as recognized.

II. Respect for Persons. The psychoanalyst is expected to treat patients and their families, students and colleagues with respect and care. Discrimination on the basis of age, disability, ethnicity, gender, race, religion, sexual orientation or socioeconomic status is ethically unacceptable.

III. Mutuality and Informed Consent. The treatment relationship between the patient and the psychoanalyst is founded upon trust and informed mutual agreement or consent. At the outset of treatment, the patient should be made aware of the nature of psychoanalysis and relevant alternative therapies. The psychoanalyst should make agreements pertaining to scheduling, fees, and other rules and obligations of treatment tactfully and humanely, with adequate regard for the realistic and therapeutic aspects of the relationship. Promises made should be honored.

   When the patient is a minor these same general principles pertain but the patient's age and stage of development should guide how specific arrangements will be handled and with whom.

IV. Confidentiality. Confidentiality of the patient's communications is a basic right and an essential condition for effective psychoanalytic treatment and research. A psychoanalyst must take all measures necessary to not reveal present or former patient confidences without permission, nor discuss the particularities observed or inferred about patients outside consultative, educational or scientific contexts. If a psychoanalyst uses case material in exchanges with colleagues for consultative, educational or scientific purposes, the identity of the patient must be sufficiently disguised to prevent identification of the individual, or the patient's authorization must be obtained after frank discussion of the purpose(s) of the presentation, other options, the probable risks and benefits to the patient, and the patient's right to refuse or withdraw consent.

V. Truthfulness. The psychoanalytic treatment relationship is founded on thoroughgoing truthfulness. The psychoanalyst should deal honestly and forthrightly with patients, patient's families in the case of those who are minors, students, and colleagues. Being aware of the ambiguities and complexities of human relationships and communications, the psychoanalyst should engage in an active process of self-monitoring in pursuit of truthful therapeutic and professional exchanges.

VI. Avoidance of Exploitation. In light of the vulnerability of patients and the inequality of the psychoanalyst-analysand dyad, the psychoanalyst should scrupulously avoid any and all forms of exploitation of patients and their families, current or former, and limit, as much as possible the role of self-interest and personal desires. Sexual relations between psychoanalyst and patient or family member, current or former, are potentially harmful to both parties, and unethical. Financial dealings other than reimbursement for therapy are unethical.

VII. Scientific Responsibility. The psychoanalyst is expected to be committed to advancing scientific knowledge and to the education of colleagues and students. Psychoanalytic research should conform to generally accepted scientific principles and research integrity and should be based on a thorough knowledge of relevant scientific literature. Every precaution should be taken in research with human subjects, and in using clinical material, to respect the patient's rights especially the right to confidentiality, and to minimize potentially harmful effects.

VIII. Safeguarding the Public and the Profession. The psychoanalyst should strive to protect the patients of colleagues and other persons seeking treatment from psychoanalysts observed to be deficient in competence or known to be engaged in behavior with the potential of affecting such patients adversely. S/he should urge such colleagues to seek help. Information about unethical or impaired conduct by any member of the profession should be reported to the appropriate committee at local or national levels.

IX. Social Responsibility. A psychoanalyst should comply with the law and with social policies that serve the interests of patients and the public. The Principles recognize that there are times when conscientious refusal to obey a law or policy constitutes the most ethical action. If a third-party or patient or in the case of minor patients, the parent(s) or guardian(s) demands actions contrary to ethical principles or scientific knowledge, the psychoanalyst should refuse. A psychoanalyst is encouraged to contribute a portion of his or her time and talents to activities that serve the interests of patients and the public good.

X. Personal Integrity. The psychoanalyst should be thoughtful, considerate, and fair in all professional relationships, uphold the dignity and honor of the profession, and accept its self-imposed disciplines. He or she should accord members of allied professions the respect due their competence.

STANDARDS APPLICABLE TO THE PRINCIPLES OF ETHICS FOR PSYCHOANALYSTS

The American Psychoanalytic Association is aware of the complicated nature of the psychoanalyst-patient relationship and the conflicting expectations of therapists and patients in contemporary society. In addition, the Association recognizes that this complexity is increased when the patient is a minor and parent(s) and guardian(s) are a natural, if changing, part of the therapeutic picture. The following ethical standards are offered as a more specific and practical guide for putting into practice the Guiding Principles. The Standards represent practices that psychoanalysts have found over time to be generally conducive to morally appropriate professional conduct. A discussion of situation-dependent guidelines and dilemmas will be presented in a separate document, a Casebook on Ethics.

I. COMPETENCE

1. Psychoanalysts are expected to work within the range of their professional competence and to refuse to assume re sponsibilities for which they are untrained.
2. Psychoanalysts should strive to keep up to date with changes in theories and techniques and to make appropriate use of professional consultations both psychoanalytic and in allied psychotherapeutic fields such as psychopharmacology.

3. Psychoanalysts should seek to avoid making claims in public presentations that exceed the scope of their competence.
4. Psychoanalysts should take steps to correct any impairment in his or her analyzing capacities and do whatever is necessary to protect patients from such impairment.

II. RESPECT FOR PERSONS AND NONDISCRIMINATION

1. Psychoanalysts should try to eliminate from their work the effects of biases based on age, disability, ethnicity, gender, race, religion, sexual orientation or socioeconomic status.
2. The psychoanalyst should refuse to observe organizational policies that discriminate with regard to age, disability, ethnicity, gender, race, religion, sexual orientation, or socioeconomic status.

III. MUTUALITY AND INFORMED CONSENT

1. Psychoanalytic treatment exists by virtue of an informed choice leading to a mutually accepted agreement between a psychoanalyst and a patient or the parent(s) or guardian(s) of a minor patient.
2. It is not ethical for a psychoanalyst to take advantage of the power of the transference relationship to aggressively solicit patients, students or supervisees into treatment or to prompt testimonials from current or former patients. Neither is it ethical to take such advantage in relation to parent(s) or guardian(s) of current or former minor patients.
3. It is unethical for a psychoanalyst to use his/her position of power in analytic organization, professional status or special relationship with a potential patient or parent or guardian of a minor patient to coerce or manipulate the person into treatment.
4. Careful attention should be given to the process of referral to avoid conflicts of interest with other patients and colleagues. Referrals between members of the same family, including spouses, and significant others, should be especially scrutinized and disclosure should be made to patients about the relationship in the initial stages of the referral so that preferable alternatives may be considered.

5. All aspects of the treatment contract which are applicable
    should be discussed with the patient during the initial con-
    sultation process. The psychoanalyst's policy of charging
    for missed sessions should be understood in advance of
    such a charge. The applications of this policy to third party
    payment for services should be discussed and agreed upon
    by the patient. In the case of patients who are minors, these
    matters should be discussed early on with the parent(s) or
    guardian(s) as well as with the patient as age and capabil-
    ity dictate.
6. A reduced fee does not limit any of the ethical responsibil-
    ities of the treating psychoanalyst.
7. The psychoanalyst should not unilaterally discontinue
    treating a patient without adequate notification and dis-
    cussion with the patient and, if a minor, with the parent (s)
    or guardian (s) and an offer of referral for further treat-
    ment. Consultation should be considered.

IV. CONFIDENTIALITY

1. All information about the specifics of a patient's life is con-
    fidential, including the name of the patient and the fact of
    treatment. The psychoanalyst should resist disclosing con-
    fidential information to the full extent permitted by law.
    Furthermore, it is ethical, though not required, for a psy-
    choanalyst to refuse legal, civil or administrative demands
    for such confidential information even in the face of the
    patient's informed consent and accept instead the legal
    consequences of such a refusal.[1]
2. The psychoanalyst should never share confidential infor-
    mation about a patient with nonclinical third-parties (e.g.,

---

[1]Refusal of such demands for confidential information, while ethical, may have
serious consequences for the patient, e.g., loss of benefits, loss of a job opportunity, etc., which may cause the patient to take some legal action against the
member. The fact that refusal is ethical is unlikely to protect the psychoanalyst
in those circumstances, unless the member has made his or her position clear
both at the onset and throughout treatment. Even with these clarifications a degree of exposure may remain.

insurance companies) without the patient's or, in the case of a minor patient, the parent's or guardian's informed consent. For the purpose of claims review or utilization management, it is not a violation of confidentiality for a psychoanalyst to disclose confidential information to a consultant psychoanalyst, provided the consultant is also bound by the confidentiality standards of these Principles and the informed consent of the patient or parent **or** guardian of a minor patient has first been obtained. If a third-party payer or a patient or parent **or** guardian of a minor patient demands that the psychoanalyst act contrary to these Principles, it is ethical for the psychoanalyst to re-fuse such demands, even with the patient's or, in the case of a minor patient, the parent's or guardian's informed consent.[2]

3. The psychoanalyst of a minor patient must seek to preserve the patient's confidentiality, while keeping parents or guardians informed of the course of treatment in ways appropriate to the age and stage of development of the patient, the clinical situation and these Principles.

4. The psychoanalyst should take particular care that patient records and other documents are handled so as to protect patient confidentiality. A psychoanalyst may direct an executor to destroy such records and documents after his or her death.[3]

5. It is not a violation of confidentiality for a psychoanalyst to disclose confidential information about a patient in a formal consultation or supervision in which the consultant or supervisor is also bound by the confidentiality require-

[2]The caveat expressed in footnote 1 is applicable. Again, the psychoanalyst may refuse the patient's demand that he or she act contrary to the Principles. While this may protect a member against accusations of unethical conduct, it is unlikely to protect a psychoanalyst against legal allegations of substandard conduct.

[3]The American Psychoanalytic Association's Ethics Committee has recommended the deletion of this sentence because of concerns that it might put practitioners at an ethical and legal risk; however, no formal action could be taken prior to this printing. For the most current version of the Ethics Principles and Standards, visit the Association's website at www.apsa.org.

ments of these Principles. On seeking consultation, the psychoanalyst should first ascertain that the consultant or supervisor is aware of and accepts the requirements of the
Confidentiality standard.

6. If the psychoanalyst uses confidential case material in clinical presentations or in scientific or educational exchanges
with colleagues, either the case material must be disguised
sufficiently to prevent identification of the patient, or the
patient's informed consent must first be obtained. If the latter, the psychoanalyst should discuss the purpose(s) of such
presentations, the possible risks and benefits to the patient's treatment and the patient's right to withhold or
withdraw consent. In the case of a minor patient, parent(s)
or guardian(s) should be consulted and, depending on the
age and developmental stage, the matter may be discussed
with the patient as well.

7. Supervisors, peer consultants and participants in clinical
and educational exchanges have an ethical duty to maintain the confidentiality of patient information conveyed for
purposes of consultative or case presentations or scientific
discussions.

8. Candidate psychoanalysts-in-training are strongly urged to
consider obtaining the patient's informed consent before
beginning treatment, pertaining to disclosures of confidential information in groups or written reports required by
the candidate's training. Where the patient is a minor, the
candidate is strongly urged to consider obtaining informed
consent from the parent(s) or guardian(s); age and stage of
development will assist the candidate in determining if the
patient should also be informed.

V. TRUTHFULNESS

1. Candidate psychoanalysts-in-training are strongly urged to
inform psychoanalytic training patients and prospective
psychoanalytic training patients that they are in training
and supervised. Where the patient is a minor, the parent(s)
or guardian(s) should also be informed. If asked, candidate

psychoanalysts-in-training should not deny that they are being supervised as a requirement of their training.

2. The psychoanalyst should speak candidly with prospective patients or the parent(s) or guardian(s) if the patient is a minor about the benefits and burdens of psychoanalytic treatment.

3. The psychoanalyst should avoid misleading patients or parents or guardians of minor patients or the public with statements that are knowingly false, deceptive or misleading.

VI. AVOIDING EXPLOITATION

1. Sexual relationships involving any kind of sexual activity between the psychoanalyst and a current or former patient, or a parent or guardian of a current or former patient, or any member of the patient's immediate family whether initiated by the patient, the parent or guardian or family member or by the treating psychoanalyst, are unethical. Physical touching is not ordinarily regarded as a technique of value in psychoanalytic treatment. If touching occurs, whether of the patient by the psychoanalyst or the psychoanalyst by the patient, such an event should alert the psychoanalyst to the potential for misunderstanding of the event by the patient or the psychoanalyst. There may be harm to the future course of treatment and consultation should be considered. Consultation should be considered if there is any concern about the future course of treatment.

   With children before the age of puberty touching between the patient and the psychoanalyst is likely to occur as in helping or during a patient's exuberant play. Also, a disruptive or out of control child may need to be restrained. The psychoanalyst needs to be alert to the multiple meanings for both parties of such touching. Keeping parent(s) or guardian(s) informed when this occurs may be useful. Consultation should be considered if the touching causes the psychoanalyst concern.

2. Marriage between a psychoanalyst and a current or former patient, or between a psychoanalyst and the parent or

guardian of a patient or former patient is unethical, notwithstanding the absence of a complaint from the spouse and the legal rights of the parties.

3. It is not ethical for a psychoanalyst to engage in financial dealings with a patient, or in the case of a minor patient, the parent(s) or guardian(s) beyond reimbursement for treatment; or to use information shared by a patient or parent(s) or guardian(s) for the psychoanalyst's financial gain.

4. It is not ethical for a psychoanalyst to solicit financial contributions from a current or former patient or the parent/guardian of a current or former patient for any purpose; nor should a psychoanalyst give the names of current or former patients or their parents/guardians for purposes of financial solicitation by others.

5. If a patient or parent or guardian of a minor patient brings up the idea of a financial gift to a psychoanalytic organization or cause during treatment, it should be handled psychoanalytically and, if necessary, the patient should be informed that his or her confidentiality might be breached by the treating psychoanalyst's obligation to recuse him/herself from involvement in decisions governing use of the gift. If a gift is given nevertheless, the psychoanalyst is ethically obliged to refrain from any decision regarding its use by the recipient organization or cause.

6. If a current or former patient or the parent/guardian of a current or former patient, gives an unsolicited financial gift, or establishes a trust or foundation or other entity for the benefit of his/her psychoanalyst, or for the benefit of the professional or scientific work of said psychoanalyst, or for the benefit of the psychoanalyst's family, or the gift is placed under the control of the psychoanalyst, even if not directly beneficial to the psychoanalyst or his/her family, it is not ethical for the psychoanalyst to accept any financial benefit or to control its disposition.

7. It is ethical for a psychoanalyst to accept a bequest from the estate of a former patient, provided that it is promptly donated to an organization or cause from which the psychoanalyst or his/her family do not personally benefit and over which the psychoanalyst has no direct control.

8. It is unethical for a psychoanalyst to use his or her professional status, special relationship, or position of power in an analytic organization to solicit gifts or funds, sexual favors, special relationships, or other tangible benefit from patients, the parent(s) or guardian(s) of minor patients, members of the patient's immediate family, psychoanalysts-in-training or supervisees. Sexual relationships between current supervisors and supervisees are unethical.

9. Concurrent supervision of candidates by the spouse, significant other or other relative of their analysts should be avoided whenever possible in the interest of maintaining the independence and objectivity of both the supervisory and analytic processes.

VII. Scientific Responsibility

1. The psychoanalyst should take every precaution in using clinical material to respect the patient's rights and to minimize the impact of its use on the patient's privacy and dignity. In the case of minor patients the impact on parent(s) or guardian(s) needs to be considered. Particular care should be exercised in using material from a patient who is still undergoing treatment.

2. It is unethical for a psychoanalyst to make public presentations or submit for publication in scientific journals falsified material that does not refer to actual observations drawn from the clinical situation. Such clinical material must be disguised sufficiently to protect identification of the patient.

3. The psychoanalyst should exercise caution in disguising patient material to avoid misleading colleagues as to the source and significance of his or her scientific conclusions.

VIII. Safeguarding the Public and the Profession

1. The psychoanalyst should seek consultation when, in the course of treating a patient, the work becomes continu-

ously confusing or seriously disturbing to either the psychoanalyst or the patient, or both. On occasion in the treatment of a minor, the relationship between the psychoanalyst and parental figure may cause sustained disturbance or confusion for the psychoanalyst. In such a situation consultation is indicated.

2. A psychoanalyst who undergoes a serious illness and extended convalescence, or whose analyzing capacities are impaired, must consult with a colleague and/or medical specialist to clarify the significance of his or her condition and its impact on continuing to work.

3. A request by a patient, a parent/guardian of a minor patient, or a colleague that the psychoanalyst seek consultation should receive respectful and reflective consideration.

4. If a psychoanalyst is officially notified by a representative of an institute or society that a possible impairment of his/her clinical judgment or analyzing ability exists, the psychoanalyst must consult with no less than two colleagues, one of whom may be a non-analyst medical specialist, each acceptable to the notifying body. If impairment is found, remedial measures be followed by the psychoanalyst in order to protect patients from harm and to prevent degradation of the standards of care in the profession.

5. It is ethical for a psychoanalyst to consult with the patient of a colleague without giving notice to the colleague, if the consultation has been requested by the patient.

6. It is ethical for a psychoanalyst to intervene on behalf of a colleague's patient if he or she has evidence from a direct or indirect consultation with the colleague's patient or from supervision of the colleague's work with the patient that the colleague may be conducting him/herself unethically toward the patient or may be so impaired as to threaten the patient's welfare.

7. It is ethical for a psychoanalyst to accept for treatment the current patient of a colleague if consultation with a third colleague indicates that it is in the best interest of the patient to do so.

8. In the event that a credible threat of imminent bodily harm

to a third party by a patient becomes evident, the psychoanalyst should take reasonable appropriate steps to protect the third-party from bodily harm, and may breach patient confidentiality if necessary only to the extent necessary to prevent imminent harm from occurring. The same applies to a credible threat of suicide.

9. In the case of a minor where the psychoanalyst is concerned that a credible threat of serious self injury or suicide is imminent, the psychoanalyst should take appropriate steps. This would include the notification of parent(s) or guardian(s) even if a breach of confidentiality is required. Under these circumstances, any breach of confidentiality should be restricted to the minimum necessary to prevent harm of the minor child.

10. When a psychoanalyst becomes convinced that abuse is occurring the psychoanalyst may report adult or child abuse of a patient or by a patient to the appropriate governmental agency in keeping with local laws. Should the patient be a minor, informing parent(s) or guardian(s) needs to be considered. In these circumstances, confidentiality may be breached to the minimum extent necessary. However, in keeping with General Principle IX, a psychoanalyst may also refuse to comply with local reporting laws if that psychoanalyst believes that to do so would seriously undermine the treatment or damage the patient. Given the complexities of these matters, a psychoanalyst who is concerned that abuse of an adult or child is occurring is encouraged to continue to explore the situation and to consider utilizing consultation to determine what course of action would be most helpful.[4]

11. Local psychoanalytic societies and institutes have an obligation to promote the competence of their members and to initiate confidential inquiries in response to ethics complaints.

[4]A refusal to comply with local reporting laws may be in the patient's best interest; however, the psychoanalyst must recognize that his/her action may result in exposure to prosecution by the government or a civil action based on these laws.

IX. SOCIAL RESPONSIBILITY

1. The psychoanalyst should make use of all legal, civil, and administrative means to safeguard patients' rights to confidentiality, to ensure the protection of patient treatment records from third party access, and to utilize any other ethical measures to ensure and maintain the privacy essential to the conduct of psychoanalytic treatment.
2. The psychoanalyst is urged to support laws and social policies that promote the best interests of patients and the ethical practice of psychoanalysis.
3. The psychoanalyst is encouraged to contribute his or her time and talents, if necessary without monetary compensation, to consultative and educational activities intended to improve public welfare and enhance the quality of life for the mentally ill and economically deprived members of the community.

X. INTEGRITY

1. Psychoanalysts and candidate psychoanalysts-in-training should be familiar with the Principles of Ethics and Standards, other applicable professional ethics codes, and their application to psychoanalysis.
2. Psychoanalysts should strive to be aware of their own beliefs, values, needs and limitations and to monitor how these personal interests impact their work.
3. Psychoanalysts should cooperate with ethics investigations and proceedings conducted in accordance with the Provision for Implementation of the Principles and Standards of Ethics for Psychoanalysts. Failure to cooperate is itself an ethics violation.

I.B

PROVISIONS FOR IMPLEMENTATION OF THE PRINCIPLES AND STANDARDS OF ETHICS FOR PSYCHOANALYSTS

I. COMMITTEE ON ETHICS: THERE SHALL BE A JOINT STANDING COMMITTEE ON ETHICS OF THE BOARD ON PROFESSIONAL STANDARDS AND THE EXECUTIVE COUNCIL.

A.   Composition and Appointment. The Committee on Ethics ("Committee") shall consist of seven members appointed jointly by the President of the Association ("President") and the Chair of the Board on Professional Standards ("Board Chair"). At least one of the seven members shall be a child analyst. Each member shall serve a staggered five year term; members will be appointed each year to replace members whose term has expired.

The President and Board Chair will jointly designate one member to act as chair of the Committee for a term of two years and, in the event of a vacancy on the Committee, will jointly appoint members to complete the unexpired term of the incumbent member. The President and the Board Chair will jointly appoint a substitute to replace any Committee member who recuses him/herself from a case or who is unable to serve for any other reason. In the event that the case involves a patient who is a minor the President and the Board Chair will assure that a child analyst will serve on the Committee. On completion of the disposition of such a case, the recused, or otherwise unavailable member shall resume his/her seat on the Committee.

B. Duties. The Committee on Ethics shall:
(1) Respond to communications regarding the "Principles and Standards of Ethics for Psychoanalysts" ("Principles") and the "Provisions for Implementation of the Principles of Ethics for Psychoanalysts" ("Provisions") and issue advisory opinions regarding the application of the "Principles" to particular conduct.
(2) Recommend to the Board on Professional Standards and the Executive Council appropriate additions or modifications to the "Principles" and "Provisions."
(3) Pursuant to procedures hereinafter described, review decisions of Affiliated Societies, Study Groups, Accredited and Provisionally Accredited Training Institutes (hereinafter, collectively, "local groups") with regard to complaints alleging that a member of the Association has breached the "Principles." Such review shall enable the Committee to (a) make a decision on the basis of the local group's investigation and decision, regarding the psychoanalyst's membership status in the Association; and (b) where appropriate, make recommendations to local groups regarding their handling and disposition of such matters.
(4) Complaints against colleagues who have no local membership will be heard by an ad hoc committee appointed by the Association President and the Chairman of the Board. Upon completion of this adjudication, the decision can be reviewed by the Ethics Committee of the American and/or appealed according to the usual procedures.

II. ASSOCIATION PROCEDURES IN REGARD TO QUESTIONS OF UNETHICAL CONDUCT

A. Advisory Opinions.
(1) Requests for advisory opinions will be referred to the Chair, Committee on Ethics for response. Copies of responses will be sent to the President and the Board Chair.

(2) The Committee will prepare summaries of any such advisory opinions rendered. Summaries will be distributed to the membership after approval by the Executive Committee or by the Board on Professional Standards and the Executive Council on referral from the Executive Committee.

B. Adjudication.
(1) A complaint alleging breach of the "Principles" by a member of the Association must be made directly to a local group.
(2) If a complaint alleging breach of the "Principles" is addressed to the Association, it shall be referred to the charged member's local group for investigation.
(3) The Association may also refer to a member's local group publicly available information about the member, including information about malpractice findings, adverse membership actions by professional societies, and loss or restriction of license, and request that the local group initiate an ethics investigation on the basis of such information.

III. ADJUDICATION AT THE LOCAL LEVEL

A.   Committee on Ethics of Local Group. Each local group shall have a Committee on Ethics for dealing with complaints of unethical conduct.

B.   Informal Proceedings and Resolution.
(1) Each local group shall consider establishing mechanisms to enable it to determine whether to proceed pursuant to formal procedures outlined in Section III below, or to address the issues through more informal, nonadversarial proceedings which can facilitate the efficient resolution of the complaint in a manner that is educational and corrective to the member.
(2) The local group's procedures should include a description of any such informal mechanisms for resolution of which the complainant may take advantage and of any early, informal procedures by which the local group may decide to resolve the complaint through alternative, informal means, rather than through formal procedures.

C.   Initial Response to Potential Complaint. The local group should furnish any potential complainant copies of the group's procedures for dealing with complaints of unethical conduct, and of the Association's "Principles" and "Provisions."

The complainant should also be informed that such complaint must identify the charged member; must be in writing and be signed by the complainant; must clearly describe the facts and circumstances surrounding the charge of unethical conduct, citing, if possible, the applicable principle(s) of ethics alleged to have been breached; and must be accompanied by a signed statement agreeing to the use of the local group's and the Association's procedures, asking that action be taken and authorizing the distribution of the complaint and other materials submitted by the complainant in connection with the investigation.

D.   Notification of Accused Member. The local group shall then notify the charged member of the complaint, providing copies of the complaint and other materials submitted by the complainant, the group's procedures for handling ethics complaints, and the Association's "Provisions."

E.   Determination of Whether Complaint Merits Investigation. The local group shall determine whether the complaint merits investigation under the ethical standards established by the "Principles," and whether it might also constitute a violation of the rules of the charged members's professional licensing board. If it does not, the complainant and the charged member shall be so informed in writing. Since the adjudication was not completed, the Committee on Ethics can not accept a request for review nor can the Association consider an appeal. If the complaint is determined to merit further investigation, the charged member shall be informed in writing and notified of the right to a hearing, and that during the investigation and hearing, the rights set out in Section (F) below shall apply.

F.   Procedures of Local Group. The local group's procedures for handling complaints of unethical conduct must assure fair process and provide the charged member with the following:

(1) the opportunity to be notified of, and to address, the charges;

(2) the right to be represented by legal counsel;

(3) the right to a hearing, including the right to call, examine and cross-examine witnesses, or reasonable alternatives thereto;

(4) notice of not less than 30 days of the date, place, and time of the hearing, the witnesses expected to testify thereat; and the member's procedural rights at the hearing;

(5) the right to submit a written statement at the end of any hearing;

(6) the right to have a record made of the hearing proceedings and to have a copy of the record upon payment of reasonable charges; and

(7) that relevant evidence will not be excluded from any hearings solely on the grounds that it would not be admissible in a court of law'

(8) the right to receive (a) the written final decision or recommendation of the ethics committee or other hearing body, including a statement of the basis therefore, and (b) if the hearing body makes a recommendation to its local group or other body of the local group, a written final decision of the group, including a statement of the basis for the decision.

G.   Decision of Local Group. In any case in which formal procedures have been followed, after full and fair consideration of the complaint and all the evidence introduced at the hearing, the local group shall arrive at a determination as to the appropriate disposition of the case. In addition to any other disposition, the local group's procedures may enable it to (1) conclude that unethical conduct may have occurred but recommend that no formal finding be made and no sanction imposed pending completion of remedial action recommended and agreed to by the charged member; or (2) dismiss the charges with prejudice, accompanying the dismissal with a letter of admonition, expressing the sense that there may be questions about the member's practices or judgment and putting the member on notice that further education, consultation and/or supervision may be indicated as well as possible sanctions.

H.   Notification of Charged Member and of American Psychoanalytic Association. After arriving at a decision, the local group shall advise the charged member, and the complainant of the action taken by the local group. If the decision of the local group is to censure, suspend or expel the charged analyst, the local group shall also notify, the President of the Association, the Chair of the Board on Professional Standards and the chair of the Committee on Ethics.

I.   Local Appeal Process. Each local group is strongly urged to establish a procedure for a local appeal of procedures to be used for investigation and/or the final local adjudication.

IV. REVIEW OF DECISION OF LOCAL GROUP AND ACTION BY ASSOCIATION

A.   Purpose of Review. The Association shall review a local group's investigation and decision in order (1) to determine whether action by the Association is appropriate, and (2) where appropriate, to make recommendations to local groups regarding their handling and disposition of the case.

B.   Circumstances of Review. The Association shall review an investigation and decision by a local group under the following circumstances:

(1.) Automatic Review. If a member of the Association has been censured, suspended, or expelled by a local group, or if his/her faculty status in an accredited Institute has been suspended or terminated as a result of adjudication of complaints of unethical conduct, a review of the case shall be promptly undertaken.

(2.) Requested Review. If the disposition of a case is other than censure, suspension or expulsion by a local group, or suspension or termination of a member's faculty status in an accredited Institute, the Association shall undertake a review of the case if formal request for such review is made to the President of the Association, by the member(s) charged, the complainant, or the local group, within 60 days after notification of the group's decision.

(a) Each such request by a complainant or charged member shall include the reasons for dissatisfaction with the action taken at the local level.

(b) Each such request by the charged member also shall include adequate information regarding the charge, and his/her defense.

(c) Each such request by a local group shall include identification of the charges and the persons involved, a description of all attempts by the group to resolve the matter, and the reason for referral to the Association.

(3) The Committee on Ethics of the American Psychoanalytic Association will not review any decision of a local group regarding a member if the Committee has already reviewed a decision regarding the same complaint or a complaint based on substantially the same facts about the member. This would have particular relevance to those societies and institutes that do not have joint ethics committees.

C. Process of Review.

(1) The initial review of the investigation and decision of a local group shall be conducted by the Association's Committee on Ethics, which may confer with the President and legal counsel of the Association.

(2) The Committee on Ethics will request all records of the investigation from the local group and will review the procedures used by the local group, its interpretation and application of the Association's "Principles" and its decision regarding the conduct complained of and any sanction imposed.

(3) In the course of its review, the Committee on Ethics may, but shall not be required to, request written briefs from complainant or counsel for complainant, charged member or counsel for the charged member, and the local group or counsel for the local group. Any brief received from the complainant or the local group shall be provided to the

charged member, who shall be given at least 30 days to respond. Personal appearance before the Committee by the complainant, charged member, or local group representatives may be requested.

(4) The Committee on Ethics shall prepare a written summary of the case, including its decision and the basis of its decision.

D. Outcome of Ethics Committee Review.

(1) On the basis of its review of the investigation and decision of the local group, the Committee, by majority vote with no more than **two** members dissenting or abstaining, shall decide what action the Association should take with regard to the complaint filed against the charged member. While based on the information gathered by the local group, the decision of the Committee on Ethics may differ from the decision arrived at by the local group. The Committee on Ethics shall vote for one of the following measures:

  (a) Exoneration. The charged member is cleared from blame as the evidence established no unethical conduct by the member.

  (b) Dismissal of Complaint Without Prejudice. This disposition permits new proceedings with respect to the same charge at a later date; i.e., when a determination on the merits cannot be made because of insufficient reliable evidence or other procedural defects.

  (c) Dismissal of Complaint With Prejudice. The complaint is dismissed without any finding of unethical conduct; proceedings with regard to the same complaint may not be reinstituted.

  Where appropriate, such a dismissal may be accompanied by a letter of admonition, expressing the sense of the Association that there may be questions about the appropriateness of the conduct of the charged member and putting the member on notice that further education, consultation and/or supervision may be indicated.

  (d) Censure.

(e) Suspension from the Association. Such suspension shall be for a stipulated period, not to exceed three years from date of suspension.

(f) Separation from the Rolls. A new application for membership in the Association shall not be entertained in less than five years from date of separation.

(g) Permanent Expulsion from the Association.

(2) On the basis of its review, the Committee may also decide to consult with the local group regarding its procedures in investigating the complaint of unethical conduct, its interpretation of the Association's "Principles" and its decision regarding the conduct complained of and sanction imposed. However, the Committee and the Association may not otherwise reverse or modify the decision of the local group.

E. Procedure Following Committee on Ethics.

(1) The Committee on Ethics shall forward a summary of the case, including a statement of the basis of its decision, to the President of the Association. The President shall notify the charged member, the complainant, and the local group of the decision and shall provide the charged member with a copy of the summary.

(2) If the decision of the Committee on Ethics has been to exonerate the charged member, to dismiss the complaint with or without prejudice, or to censure the charged member, the charged member also shall be advised that such decisions of the Committee are final, and unappealable.

(3) If the decision of the Committee on Ethics has been to suspend, separate from the rolls, or expel the charged member, the decision is not final unless it has been ratified by the Executive Council pursuant to the procedures set out in Section IV(E)(4), below. When the President notifies the charged member of such a decision, the President also shall notify the member that he/she must indicate in writing within 30 days from the date of mailing of the notice, that he/she either accepts the decision or that he/she wishes to appeal it. Unless written notification from the charged

member is received within the specified time, the right to
appeal shall have been forfeited.

(4) Executive Council Ratification or Appeal. Following notification of all parties as set out above, the Chair of the
Committee on Ethics shall present the case and its conclusions to the Executive Council sitting in Executive Session.

(a) When Appeal Not Requested. When the charged
member has not requested an appeal, The Executive
Council shall decide whether or not to ratify the decision of the Committee on Ethics.

(i) If the Executive Council by majority vote, decides
to ratify the decision of the Committee on Ethics,
the decision will be final. The Executive Council
may prepare its own written decision of the case
or adopt the conclusions of the Committee on
Ethics as the decision of the Association.

(ii) If the Council fails to ratify the decision of the
Committee on Ethics, the Council may refer the
matter back to the Committee on Ethics for further deliberation and may specify questions or
concerns it has about the matter.

(iii) If the Executive Council refers the matter back to
the Committee on Ethics, the Committee shall reconsider its decision, following procedures set
forth in Sections IV(C), (D) and (E). The President
shall notify all concerned parties of the Council's
decision, provide the charged member with current status of the matter and remind the member
of his/her right to appeal as set out in IV(E)(3). If
the charged member does not exercise the right to
appeal, the matter will again be presented for
Executive Council consideration as set out herein.

(iv) On the Executive Council's ratification of the decision of the Committee on Ethics, whether at initial or subsequent presentations, the charged
member, complainant and local group shall be notified of its decision. The charged member shall be
provided a copy of the final decision.

(b) When Appeal Requested; Executive Council Ratification. If the charged member exercises his/her right to appeal the decision of the Committee on Ethics, the President and Board Chair shall jointly appoint an Executive Council Ethics Appeals Committee consisting of five members, including at least two Councilors-at-Large, and at least one Executive Councilor. The remaining two members shall be former members of the Committee on Ethics. If the case involves a minor patient the Appeals Committee must include a child analyst. The appointment and composition of the Ethics Appeals Committee shall be confirmed by a majority vote of the Executive Council. This Committee is empowered to act on behalf of the Executive Council in adjudicating the charged member's appeal, and its decision shall be final. The Committee shall review the record of the proceedings to ascertain that proper procedures have been followed. If it deems further fact finding is required, it shall refer the matter to the Committee on Ethics for the necessary further investigation and deliberation. On completion of its further review of the matter, the Committee on Ethics shall report its decision on reconsideration of the matter to the Ethics Appeals Committee. A majority vote of this Committee shall be required to reach a final disposition of the matter. This Committee's final disposition shall be reported to Council and its report shall be considered an action by Council without further debate or vote by Council.

V. CONFIDENTIALITY AND DISCLOSURE

All information and records pertaining to a charge of unethical conduct against a member, its investigation and any decision rendered shall be kept confidential except as set forth herein. Disclosure is authorized in the following instances:

A. Information may be disclosed to those members, staff and non-member consultants who need the information to assure the effective administration of these procedures.

B. A decision relating to a charge of unethical conduct, which has been reviewed and ratified by the Executive Council:

   (1) shall be reported with identification of the member, to the Meeting of Members in the Secretary's report of the Minutes of the Executive Council and in such written Minutes, circulated by mail to the membership of the Association if the decision has resulted in the suspension, separation from the rolls, or expulsion of the member from the Association;

   (2) shall be reported to the membership of the Association as noted in V(B)(1) above if the decision has resulted in the censure of the member, with the identification of the member included only at the discretion of the Executive Council; and

   (3) shall be reported, to the membership of the Association as noted above, if the decision has been to dismiss the charges or exonerate the member, with the identification of the member only on his/her written request.

C. The Committee on Ethics may, at its discretion, report decisions or disclose other matters brought before it to other components of the Association, provided the identity of the parties involved is not revealed.

D. The Committee on Ethics shall provide information concerning a charge of unethical conduct, including the name of the charged member, to the Association's Membership Committee and the Board's Certification Committee when either of these committees consider an application from a member who has been sanctioned for unethical conduct. This information should also be supplied to the Appointments Committee chairs of the Board and Council.

E. The Committee on Ethics may disclose a decision concerning a charge of unethical conduct to other appropriate ethical bodies or, when required by law, to appropriate governmental or other entities.

F. The Executive Council may report an ethics complaint or a decision finding that a member has acted unethically to any licensing authority, professional society or other entity or person if it considers such disclosure appropriate to protect the public.

VI. RESIGNATION

The Association shall not be required to accept a resignation from a member against whom a charge of unethical conduct is pending. An offer of resignation, whether or not it is accepted by the Association, shall not require the termination of an investigation of unethical conduct, nor prevent the rendering or disclosure of a decision on such a charge.

VII. INDEMNIFICATION

As a condition of membership in the Association, each member agrees to cooperate with the work of the Committee on Ethics, on request, and to release, hold harmless and indemnify the Association, its officers, agents and members of the Committee on Ethics from any and all claims:

A. arising out of the institution and processing of investigations of unethical conduct in respect to said member, and the imposition and disclosure of sanctions as a result of such proceedings; and

B. with respect to any third party action or proceeding brought against such member based upon, relying on, arising from or with reference to the Principle of Ethics and Standards of the Association or any ethical proceeding conducted by the Association involving such member.

II
INTRODUCTION TO THE AMERICAN PSYCHOANALYTIC ASSOCIATION CASE BOOK ON ETHICS

The newly revised American Psychoanalytic Association Principles and Standards develops a general code of appropriate ethical behavior applicable to the practice of psychoanalysis and psychoanalytic psychotherapy. The code provides ten guiding principles and then elaborates some of the items under each principle. The standards represent practices that psychoanalysts have found to be generally conducive to ethically appropriate professional conduct.

However, in the actual clinical situation between the therapist and patient during psychoanalytic treatment, ethical issues and dilemmas become more complex as situation-dependent variables begin to emerge. The increased flexibility and variety of acceptable analytic techniques in recent decades adds to the complexity of clinical judgment. Additionally, techniques once seen as acceptable may be considered unethical by current standards. Furthermore, application of these principles to the practice of child and adolescent analysis must take into consideration the techniques and developmental issues that have evolved in that arena.

At times conflicting ethical principles coexist, requiring the analyst to recognize the implications of various solutions in order to make informed choices. It is imperative that institutes, societies and individual practitioners become more aware of and responsive to ethical issues. The establishment of a standing Psychoanalyst Assistance Committee is now mandated for each group.

Ethical issues and legal issues may also at times be in conflict, making judgments even more complex. Differences between federal and state laws and between various state legal codes further compound the situation. This makes it necessary for analysts to be familiar with the legal requirements of the state or county in which they practice. What is ethical in keeping with this code may not protect the analyst from legal action or consequences.

SOME OF THE FACTORS EMPHASIZING THIS NEED AT THIS TIME ARE AS FOLLOWS:

1. Awareness that ethical violations and boundary crossings have occurred more frequently than previously acknowledged, and that these violations have serious negative effects on the reputation of the profession in public opinion.
2. Consciousness raising and prevention are easier and less expensive to implement than handling a violation after it has occurred. Ethical violations result in significant damage to the analysand, the analyst, and the psychoanalytic community.
3. Awareness and concepts of professional ethics have become much more sophisticated and are not limited to sanctions for "bad behavior".
4. Increasing recognition of the role of the analyst's behavior in the development and maintenance of analytical process, and the analyst's countertransference, reinforcing the continuing need for self observation.
5. The need to demonstrate to colleagues, students and the general community the importance that is given to ethical issues by psychoanalytic institutions.
6. The increasingly litigious nature of society and the mounting frequency of malpractice lawsuits.
7. The importance of open discussion and sharing of ethical concerns and differences of opinion, so that a consensus about ethical behaviors becomes an expectable part of the professional climate.

For these reasons, the committee that revised the code of
ethical standards has sought to expand awareness of these issues through stimulating formal educational offerings in psychoanalytic and psychodynamic psychotherapy curricula and
also has promoted the development of discussion groups at local and national meetings. The experience during these various
educational programs has been that specific illustrations of the
general principles seem to be the most effective tool for raising
awareness of the subtleties and complexities of many ethical issues, and that clinical vignettes stimulate productive discussion.

The committee therefore has put together this book of case
vignettes on ethics with the intention of providing clinical illustrations which will serve to initiate individual and group
thought and discussion and raise awareness of the importance
of ethical behavior in the psychoanalytic situation. Some of the
lengthier cases illustrate patterns of thinking and methodology
for confronting ethical dilemmas. Integration of ethics, clinical
implications, and legal requirements may be a complex and
difficult task, but we believe that increased awareness of these
complexities will assist analysts in comfortably carrying out
their professional activities.

The vignettes offered in this collection are either hypothetical, generic or composites that illustrate some of the subtleties
and conflicts with which we must deal in practice. All names
are fictitious and do not identify any persons either living or
deceased.

III

CASE VIGNETTES AND DISCUSSION OF ISSUES IN APPLYING PRINCIPLES OF ETHICS TO CLINICAL PRACTICE*

A. PSYCHOANALYTIC COMPETENCE

All psychoanalysts do not begin practice with equal competence. This is generally true of professional individuals whose skills and abilities are a function of multiple variables. There is a consensus that following graduation from an analytic institute, it takes people several years of independent practice to fully develop optimal psychoanalytic competence. The expectation is that analysts will achieve an average level of competence as a baseline. From this point, growth in understanding and skill in practicing will enhance an individual's competence. Keeping up with current developments in theory and practice, including the use of medication in psychoanalysis, is part of maintaining competence. Continuous self-assessment is expected of the mature professional and is an essential part of an analyst's self care.

The psychoanalyst's self assessment may vary from positive and essentially confident levels of function to periods of

*The editors would like to express their appreciation to Julian Clark for his help in the electronic preparation of the vignettes and discussion section of this book.

1

uncertainty and doubt. Analysts should be aware that on some occasions they are more in tune with the analytic process and situation than at other times. The hope is that each person will be reasonably objective and will be capable of recognizing a need for
consultation when their analytic competence is significantly compromised. This recognition may result from self observation or it
may become apparent to peers, students, analysands or others.
The manifestations of a significant decline in the individual's capacity to function may vary, but sooner or later a significant decline will have to be dealt with either by the self- observing analyst
or by others.

Most psychoanalysts complete their training at a later
stage of life than other professionals, and for many this may
lead to a wish to continue to practice beyond the usual retirement age. This may contribute to a strong tendency to deny the
deleterious effects of aging, disability and illness. Self scrutiny
may fail. and then other means must be employed to assure
that practicing psychoanalysts are competent and equal to the
complicated challenges of their position.

An ethical approach to psychoanalyst illness, aging and disability is fraught with conflicting priorities. The primary concern
should be for patient protection but what happens when the doctor is also a patient? When illness suddenly strikes, or disability
and aging gradually impair functioning, the psychoanalyst is introduced to a new world of sensation and perception. This is usually
unpleasant and may even be threatening enough to foster regres-
sion. This is a common reaction that is maladaptive at a time when
complex decisions must be made that call for the utmost in matu-
rity and careful thinking.

Consultation with a trusted colleague or designated group
would be helpful but very often the psychoanalysts who are in
need of help retreat into denial and disavow their need. Secrecy
and isolation from the community usually follows denial.
There is often the feeling that if one is perceived to be ill or disabled, then economic punishment will follow in the form of
lack of referrals. Thus the isolation and secrecy can be rationalized as self-protective. Decision-making about how to handle
the illness or disability both personally and therapeutically
then proceeds without outside help and independent insights.

Analytic colleagues and friends usually do not wish to see deterioration in a peer. They also tend to identify with the impaired person thus contributing to a communal denial. Patients, students and supervisees may also have their own need to deny the disturbing facts. The combination of a regressive self-interest on the part of the analyst and a strong tendency towards distortion in a transference-blinded patient, student or supervisee can lead to mutual denial and serious acting out of fantasy. The analyst does not want to lose his or her youth, competence and health, and the patient or student does not want to lose his or her analyst or teacher.

Who should make the judgment that there is a problem of competence? The consequences of such an evaluation may create significant and painful distress both for the individual analysts involved as well as for the institutional structures of the psychoanalytic community.

Even when ethical guidance is sought, it may not be easily available. There are shockingly few resources currently available to offer ethical guidance and support and those that are available may be avoided by the ill, disabled or aging analyst.

The new ethics guidelines call for a Psychoanalyst Assistance Committee to be established in each psychoanalytic society and/or institute. This group would be available to hear from people with concerns about analytic competence and to informally look at the possible problem areas with the intention of mediating any disputes or misunderstandings and preventing harmful consequences. This is an area which calls for our most careful thinking and our most tactful and humane implementation efforts. There is a communal responsibility towards each other and to the community at large which can be best assumed by local groups.

COMPETENCE / Temporary Illness (A-1-a)

Dr. Alfred goes for a routine physical exam and is found to have cancer. Believing that honesty is the best policy he tells his patients that he has a treatable cancer and will be taking off a few months for surgery and other treatments. His colleagues are privy to the same information.

When he returns to practice several months later he is dismayed to find that some patients do not return and furthermore, that no new referrals are forthcoming from colleagues. He had been honest with referral sources and felt that since he had recovered enough to work that he was deserving of the usual consideration. Besides, he had not worked in some time and was eager to return for professional self esteem as well as financial need.

You have a possible referral for Dr. Alfred but the patient will probably need long term treatment. You don't know whether to believe Dr. Alfred in his optimism. Should you defer referrals until time proves him cured? How much time would convince you that he is okay? Should you discuss your concerns and this decision with Dr. Alfred?

COMPETENCE / Temporary Illness (A-1-b)

Dr. Stephens was noted by colleagues to be increasingly sallow in his complexion, feeble in his physical motor movements and intermittently confused and uncertain of his orientation. On one occasion he asked a colleague where the door to his office was. The students in the class that he was teaching reported that he seemed much less alert and at times was unresponsive to the questions that were presented to him in connection with the assigned reading.

Eventually the director of the Institute recommended to the chairperson of the Psychoanalyst Assistance Committee that the committee contact Dr. Stephens to express the concerns and suggest an evaluation.

The chair of the committee contacted Dr. Stephens and requested a meeting with two committee members. At that meeting Dr. Stephens was told about the concerns and observations of individuals in the analytic community. He was asked to undergo a full medical and psychological evaluation as soon as possible, to be conducted by Dr. Stephens' own physician, and by a neuropsychologist chosen by the committee. Although Dr.

Stephens was distressed by this request he agreed to cooperate since his faculty reappointment was conditional upon his following up on such a requirement.

Several weeks later the chair of the PAC received a report from the psychologist who had been consulted by Dr. Stephens to the effect that he seemed to be experiencing a significant fluctuating organic brain syndrome. At the same time he also received a report from Dr. Stephens' internist indicating that Dr. Stephens was suffering from late onset, but severe, diabetes mellitus and that he had begun a regimen of diet and insulin to control the diabetes. The prognosis was said to be good and the internist indicated he would continue with Dr. Stephens' treatment.

Within about ten days, Dr. Stephens began to be more animated, active, and responsive and appeared significantly more energetic, functioning at his previous level, and he seemed again to be "his old self."

DISCUSSION

This vignette illustrates the importance of recognizing difficulty or disability in colleagues and teachers and having a systematic response in place to deal with this recognition. Although painful and sometimes shocking to the people involved, confronting the situation allows the possibility that the disability could be reversible with effective treatment. The evaluation revealed the previously undiagnosed diabetes that was causing the problem. The treatment was effective and not only restored his functioning but prevented what would have certainly been further and probably irreversible deterioration. The procedure was not adversarial and was promptly activated since it was already established and familiar to the faculty.

COMPETENCE / TEMPORARY ILLNESS (A-1-c)

Dr. Bloom finds out that his chronic abdominal distress is due to a benign tumor which has to be surgically removed. He schedules the surgery for his summer vacation and decides to maintain his privacy by not telling the situation to patients. He also refrains from telling most colleagues, except for his closest friends. But word gets around that he has a serious illness and the absence of information seems to fuel the rumors.

One of Dr. Bloom's patients consults you and wishes to continue treatment with you requesting that you not communicate with Dr. Bloom about the situation. The patient is convinced that the rumors he heard were only the tip of the iceberg and that Dr. Bloom must be in a very unstable medical situation.

You have different and more reassuring news. Do you offer this information? Are you obligated to try to get the patient to return to Dr. Bloom?

COMPETENCE / PROGRESSIVE ILLNESS (A-2)

Dr. Les Wiser learns that he has a chronic neurological illness which will gradually affect both mind and body. No signs of the illness would be apparent to a casual observer at this time and he feels quite well but he has been told that he will eventually become incapacitated. He would like to continue working but also wants to be ethically responsible and not do any harm. After some consideration he decides to handle his problem in the following manner.

He decides to keep his illness to himself for the most part and not tell anything to his patients. Since he had planned to retire in the next few years he decides to quietly move up his retirement by accepting only short term referrals. While maintaining his very considerable personal fortitude, he evaluates his patients in terms of how rapidly he can terminate their treatment. His goal is to complete the treatment of his existing cases without revealing his condition or the reasons for this decision. He feels that he is making a considerable sacrifice to maintain the integrity of the treatment of his existing case load and that his exit will be in the tradition of physicianly self sacrifice. This is a comfort to him and a source of self esteem as he faces a discouraging personal future.

Dr. Wiser does confide in a very few friends and colleagues. Should they respond with admiration or can they come up with a better strategy for him? He cannot imagine that his reasoned response will be criticized and he does not think that personal psychotherapy or supervision is necessary at this time.

DISCUSSION

Dr. Wiser is mistaken about the intactness of his functioning and his self assessment that his illness does not interfere with his working with patients. While his ethical intent seems genuine, it is well known that many people have a strong tendency to deny the effects of illness and that physicians have a tendency to do this more than most people. His thought that he could rapidly terminate with some patients is an indication of his already impaired thinking.

His friends and colleagues can respond with admiration for his sense of concern for his patients, but they also have an ethical obligation to advise him to consult with someone not personally involved in order to consider his options.

This advice may be refused but perhaps his own sense of ethical responsibility can be enlarged to include some self doubt and the need for such a consultation. His friends can offer their support for this course of action. They also have an obligation to provide support if the evaluation indicates problems in competence, and to explore ways that he can remain active in the professional community within his limitations. It would certainly seem that some supervision of his practice would be in order, both to protect his patients and to protect Dr. Wiser from his need to delude himself.

It is also ethically important to have repeated evaluations if the illness is progressive, even if a consultation reveals that there is no immediate problem with competent functioning.

Personal psychotherapy can also be supported as a way to help him make ethically appropriate decisions, as well as to help him deal with this crisis in his personal life.

COMPETENCE / Recurrent Illness (A-3)

Dr. Corelli, a 53-year-old analyst had been having occasional anginal attacks which responded promptly to nitroglycerine. One time, the attack had lasted longer and had been accompanied by an irregular heartbeat. An angiogram was recommended, and Dr. Corelli was out of his office for 3 days. He indicated to his patients that he was having some "medical tests" but did not offer any further information.

The cardiac arrhythmia recurred unexpectedly several times during the following year. On each occasion, the patients would arrive at his office to be told by the receptionist that their appointment had been canceled for that day and that Dr. Corelli would contact them as soon as possible to establish the next appointment The patients were increasingly concerned about the recurrent absences, particularly since they were unanticipated, and they pressed Dr. Corelli for further information. He then indicated that he was having recurrent episodes of cardiac arrhythmia, that these could not be anticipated but that he expected to continue actively to practice analysis.

On one occasion, Dr. Corelli entered the hospital for an angioplasty which necessitated his absence from practice for an entire week. Six months later, with a recurrence of the angina and the arrhythmia, he underwent open heart surgery with a coronary bypass, necessitating an absence from practice for approximately three months.

When he returned to practice, he indicated to the patients that his condition had been definitively treated, that he had successfully recuperated from the bypass surgery, and that he did not anticipate any further interruptions because of his health.

Should Dr. Corelli's cardiac problem make him question his competence for analytic practice? What information should Dr. Corelli provide for his analysands? Should he consider retiring from practice? If not, what information should he give to new patients? How would you deal with the issues of referral of patients to Dr. Corelli?

COMPETENCE / DYING (A-4)

You are serving as the ombudsman of the local psychoanalytic society and are approached by a psychoanalytic candidate who is in training analysis with a senior analyst. Over the past few months the analysand has noticed that his analyst is losing weight, appears increasingly pale and feeble and is having difficulty breathing. He has mentioned these observations, and the analyst's response has been to interpret negative transference and death wishes related to the death of the analysand's father.

The analysand has spoken informally to faculty members but has been told that he should take up his concerns about his analyst's health in his analysis. No one wants to deal with this issue, although obviously, many people have noticed the analyst's condition.

As ombudsman you ask the director of the institute about the analyst's health and are told that the observations made by the candidate are valid and that the analyst is terminally ill with a progressive cancer. He wishes to continue to practice as long as possible and wishes to keep this information confidential. The director, a close friend of the afflicted analyst, has postponed doing anything but now the issue is forced.

DISCUSSION

There are many ethical concerns here that are in conflict with each other. The issue is how can they be reconciled so that the analyst and the candidate are both given proper consideration so that they are both treated fairly.

From the candidate's viewpoint, his analyst is being evasive about a reality in his life. This evasion goes beyond the analyst's right to the protection of his privacy since this reality will impact severely upon the analysis. The analyst will become progressively sicker and eventually unable to continue to work. He wishes to continue as long as possible and may even regard his continuing to work as a kind of lifeline for himself, but will this benefit be at the candidate's expense? He is certainly putting his own needs above those of his patient. While the inter-

pretations about the analysand's aggression may be correct, they are only part of the total picture. An intellectually correct interpretation made in an ethical vacuum is not only not useful but likely to be damaging. This situation, in which the analyst is disregarding his patient's need for continuity and validation of his observations, is heading towards a disaster.

From the analyst's point of view, he may rationalize continuing to work without dealing with his illness by denying the severity of his condition. Some analysts are so invested in their work that they cannot imagine living without analyzing. He may also feel that his knowledge of his patient is so comprehensive that a few months more with him, even if he cannot complete the work, is valuable enough to compensate for what will be a traumatic interruption. He may even feel that as a dying person he has the right to help himself maintain his quality of life for as long as possible. All of these factors may contribute to the continuing of a basically untenable analytic situation.

Given that other faculty at the institute have noticed the analyst's decline, it is possible to take a stance of avoidance of intervention because of the general reluctance to interfere in another's business. Passing the buck is the operative mode.

What about the responsibility of the ombudsman? Perhaps his responsibility began several months earlier when he should have first noticed the incapacity of this analyst. It is tempting to ignore perceptions of a colleague's incapacity and to be reluctant to breach privacy. But at this time there is a real situation which might result in an injustice being done to a patient, whether the patient is a candidate or not. Although the ombudsman is the conduit for the expression of concern, there is a group responsibility of the analytic community to address issues of incompetence. It seems clear that some intervention should be made to allow the patient to transfer to another analyst at an appropriate time. It would be gratifying to avoid an injustice and also to prevent harm to other patients, but what about the effect of an intervention on the analyst's health and well being? This could be devastating to him.

It would be helpful if some mechanism were in place to implement the transfer with minimum trauma. The analyst must be helped to see that his denial of reality is in fact a time bomb and exploitative of the patient. This will be a painful task but it must be done to avoid a destructive outcome. Support for a colleague in trouble should be the operative mode, rather than an attitude of punishment for inappropriate behavior.

COMPETENCE / AGING (A-5-a)

Dr. Jackson. had always appeared youthful and attractive, but lately her friends and colleagues have noticed that she is very forgetful and even has totally missed some important events at which she was expected. When these omissions are gently called to her attention by friends, she always has a good reason to explain her state of distraction.

Not wishing to cause her distress, friends have covered for her at times. Her office mate has even tried to explain away a few occasions when she entirely forgot and did not show up for patient appointments. There is growing consternation and embarrassment among her friends and colleagues but no one seems to know what to do. In committee meetings her opinions are politely disregarded.

You are called by others and asked to handle the situation. What do you think you should do? What do you think you can do?

What are the responsibilities of the individual analysts who are aware of Dr. Jackson's difficulties? What should the psychoanalytic society do? How could a standing Psychoanalyst Assistance Committee be helpful?

COMPETENCE / AGING (A-5-b)

Dr. Garcia is a senior, venerated training analyst. His patient (a candidate) has, with the help of Dr. Garcia, referred his wife to you for analysis.

After an uneventful period, the wife begins to report from the couch that her husband strongly suspects that Dr. Garcia is losing his cognitive capacity. He appears confused at times, is very forgetful and even once set a small fire in a wastebasket by mistakenly throwing away a lit cigar.

You have noticed some slippage in your own contacts with Dr. Garcia but have so far disregarded the clues that indicate his growing incapacity. It is depressing to think of that brilliant mind going down the drain and you don't want it to happen.

Your patient tells you that she has urged her husband to confront his analyst with his observations. He gingerly started to do this once, and Dr. Garcia flew into a rage and threatened to report unfavorably on the progress of the analysis. He accused the candidate of being both ungrateful and unanalyzable.

Your patient wants to go to someone at the institute who can do something, since her husband is afraid to do anything else for fear of further antagonizing his analyst.

What should you do with this information? What are your responsibilities for the patient's confidentiality? What about confidentiality for the patient's husband? What are your concerns about safeguarding the public and the profession?

What if the patient's transference to you is influencing her account? What are the institute's responsibilities?

COMPETENCE / LIFE STRESS (A-6-a)

Dr. Patel is a dedicated and responsible psychoanalyst whose practice is large, and he has the reputation of being a compassionate, sincere and dedicated clinician. He is married and has two children, ages seven and nine. He is devoted to his wife and family.

His younger daughter was recently seriously injured when she was struck by a car while riding her bicycle. She suffered a major head injury and is now comatose. During the first two days of the daughter's hospitalization, Dr. Patel canceled all of his appointments in order to be with his daughter at the hospital. Subsequently, when the daughter showed no appreciable change in her condition, he felt obligated to return to his practice as quickly as possible and to be available to continue the treatment of his various analytic patients who were in various stages of transference distress in regard to his cancellations. He tried to maintain his attention to the patients and their psychological difficulties, but he frequently found himself preoccupied with concerns about his daughter. He found himself increasingly irritated by the patients' various complaints which he felt to be relatively inconsequential in comparison to his current family crisis. On one occasion, he found himself tearful and silently struggling with his irritation towards the patient in the current session and ended the session ten minutes early, not recognizing his mistake until after the patient had left.

Is this an ethical question? Should Dr. Patel inform his patients as to why he might be less attentive than usual? Should he cancel his appointments until further notice dependent on the nature of the daughter's recovery? Should he refer his patients to a "caretaker" analyst to be seen in his absence? Should he try to maintain his commitment to the patients in spite of his own stress and difficulty?

COMPETENCE / Life Stress (A-6-b)

Dr. Strauss is happily married and has two adolescent children. His wife of twenty-two years was recently found, on a routine chest x-ray, to have significant evidence of metastatic cancer, probably from her ovary; and her prognosis for health and ultimate recovery is said to be poor. Dr. Strauss is devastated by this new development and is deeply torn between his clinical responsibilities to his patients and his familial responsibility to his increasingly disabled wife and his wish to support and be with her as much as possible.

The oncologist caring for her is recommending a major and intensive course of chemotherapy and radiation which will be traumatic but is thought to be the only hope for arresting the disease. Dr. Strauss will repetitively but irregularly have to cancel many of his analytic sessions in order to accompany his wife to her treatments and also to assume greater care and responsibility in running the home.

What should Dr. Strauss do about his practice? On the one hand he needs to maintain his professional identity for his own sense of equilibrium, and yet he is aware that he cannot function at optimal effectiveness as an analyst with his patients. He is also anticipating increased financial burden from his wife's illness and treatment and needs all the income he can get from his professional work; yet he feels distressed that he is charging patients when his capacity to function is not optimal. How does he balance his own personal and emotional needs with the needs of his patients for continuity and the continuation of their therapeutic analyses? What realistic information should he offer to the patients in regard to whatever decision he makes?

DISCUSSION

Ethical and technical issues are both of concern in this situation. Most important, however, is how Dr. Strauss assesses the impact on himself and how he uses that assessment to make decisions about his own legitimate needs and the most desirable approaches to patient care.

He must first recognize that both his emotional and physical availability are likely to be compromised and that his capacity for objective self observation is at risk. Consultation at an early stage would be very helpful in monitoring his own reactions and leading to a more objective and ethical approach to decision making. For obvious reasons the consultant who is chosen to help in patient care decisions should not be a close friend, although close friends may be used for support.

Severe stress often leads to increased use of denial and rationalization. Many analysts try to immerse themselves in work when overwhelmed by external stress. Dr. Strauss may become vulnerable to countertransference enactments. For example, because Dr. Strauss cannot save his wife, he may try to compensate by extraordinary efforts with his patients. Professional identity may become a rock to which to the analyst clings in the storm. The needs of the actual patient may get lost during the process, leading to exploitation of the patient for the analyst's benefit. Inappropriate behaviors may occur, such as personal disclosures in order to elicit sympathy and support from

*the patient. Regular consultation would certainly help to iden-
tify and contain these responses. It also could provide needed
support during this period of personal devastation.*

*Dr. Strauss could certainly decide to continue practice for
many reasons including patient and personal benefit, but a review
of his caseload with help from an outside source would be ethically and technically desirable. As he continues to work, the issues
of truthfulness, mutuality and informed consent come into play. It
is not easy to decide what and when to tell patients about the future which will likely include disruptions of schedule and unanticipated absences. Patients must know enough to make an informed
choice about continuing in these circumstances, and yet should
not feel pressured to continue to support the analyst in his distress.
Truthfulness requires that Dr. Strauss not mislead his patients,
and good technique requires that he not unduly burden them with
his problem. It may be best for some analysands to be referred,
and in those cases Dr. Strauss must help them to move on by dealing with their anxiety and sense of abandonment during a transitional period. His clinical awareness and technical skills will help
him to maintain ethical behavior as he balances his own and his
patients' best interests.*

*If he plans to continue in a curtailed practice he should
explain that circumstances might require disruptions of
schedule, often with little notice. He should then give careful
attention to the impact of the changed analytic situation. He
should monitor with a consultant both his own level of competency and analysands' reactions to the new conditions. If
he decides to withdraw from practice, he could inform his patients that the demands of a personal or family situation require his full attention for an unknown time period. Ethically
he should explain his withdrawal and help the patients into
another treatment during a transitional period, giving them
time to deal with issues of guilt and abandonment.*

COMPETENCE / LIFE STRESS (A-6-c)

Dr. King is in the midst of an unpleasant, acrimonious and
bitter divorce from his wife of fourteen years. They have three

small children and he is torn about the custody issues. He feels that his wife is unfit to be the full custodial parent and, at the same time, that his goal is to minimize the psychological trauma to the children from the bitterness between himself and his wife. This situation has been developing over the past three or four months, but in the last month or so, Dr. King is increasingly discouraged, depressed, sleepless, and finding it difficult to maintain attention during analytic sessions. Given the difficulties in the legal system and the intensity of the conflict between the divorcing parties, it is likely that this situation will continue for many months and that Dr. King's difficulties in maintaining his usual analytic capacities will be even more intensely taxed as the court date approaches. Dr. King is aware that his difficult personal problem is interfering with his optimal psychoanalytic abilities and is also aware that he is frequently comparing his patients' difficulties to those he is undergoing himself.

Is this an ethical problem? Does Dr. King's increasing difficulty in maintaining his analytic listening constitute a form of temporary impairment of function? Should he struggle to continue his practice? Should he indicate to his patients what the difficulties are and suggest an interruption of their treatment? Should he refer his patients to other colleagues during the remainder of his divorce proceedings? Several colleagues are aware of his personal distress and are asking whether the Psychoanalyst Assistance Committee should become involved.

COMPETENCE / Maintaining Competence (A-7-a)

The patient, a college student seemed to be doing well in psychoanalysis but tended periodically to go into depressions that resolved within a few weeks. Interpretations did not seem to relieve these depressions but since they did go away and there was considerable analytic progress, they were not of great concern until the patient went into a depression that worsened rapidly. The patient became progressively less able to function, missed work and school, lost thirty pounds, and just lay on the couch silently or complained of feelings of pain and paralysis. This went on for weeks while her life fell apart. Her family became increasingly worried and, mindful of the strong family history of depression, began to suggest to the patient that she tell her analyst about this history and that perhaps a psychopharmacological consult be considered so that medication could be added to the treatment.

The patient brought this up in the analysis, but the analyst discouraged this idea, feeling that with time this depression would resolve as had the others. She also wished to protect the analysis by not introducing a splitting of the transference.

The situation went from bad to worse. The analyst felt that these manifestations of depression, withdrawal and negativity were related to issues which had been repeatedly interpreted but remained unresolved, and she told the patient that there was nothing more that she could do.

Finally the patient, who was now nonfunctional, had to be hospitalized. She recovered with the help of medications. The analyst, wishing to preserve the patient's privacy and confidentiality, never spoke to the hospital staff although attempts to contact her were made by them.

What are the analyst's ethical and legal responsibilities in such a situation? Is the reluctance to use medication a sign of the analyst maintaining an outmoded technical model? What is your reaction to the analyst's refusal to respond to the hospital staff? Should the analyst have sought consultation? What about education in recent developments in mental health practice?

DISCUSSION

The analyst is ethically responsible to assure that a patient receives the optimum treatment he or she needs. An analyst also has an obligation to keep up to date with the literature on other treatments; so there is sufficient familiarity to know when they are indicated. Part of this obligation includes obtaining consultation when needed. While confidentiality is important, when the analyst is one member of a treatment team such as when a patient is hospitalized, the analyst needs to be able to communicate with others on the team. This would or-

dinarily require obtaining the patient's consent. If the analyst does not attempt to obtain consent and to communicate with the treatment team if consent is given, the analyst has abandoned the patient. Protection of privacy may be assured by discretion in the information provided, but should not be used as a rationalization to avoid contact.

COMPETENCE / MAINTAINING COMPETENCE (A-7-b)

The patient was a young man who had always experienced mood swings. These occurred during the course of his analysis and usually resolved fairly quickly. They did not seem to impede the progress in his analysis until he began to have cyclical moods that were so rapid and severe that his job was affected and his life began to be disrupted. There was a family history of bipolar disorder. The patient brought up the idea of medication, but the analyst was reluctant to resort to this means of treatment. He interpreted repeatedly but did not see any improvements and finally referred the patient to a colleague in the same psychoanalytic institute who was licensed to prescribe medication.

The initial medication was not effective. The consultant advised waiting patiently for results, although it was apparent that the patient was deteriorating. Although his primary interest was not psychopharmacology, and there were many more experienced psychopharmacologists available, the consultant did not seek advice. The analyst, who was of the opinion that this was an enactment of transference fantasies, did not focus his attention on the failure of the psychopharmacological intervention.

Eventually the destructive effects of the patient's cyclical mood swings led to loss of his job and he could no longer afford to continue to see either doctor.

DISCUSSION

There are several ethical issues involved here. First, the analyst waited a very long time before referring the patient for a psychopharmacology consultation, even though it is well established that patients with bipolar disorder usually require medication. Second, the patient's condition continued to worsen even after the first mood stabilizer had been prescribed. When a patient is deteriorating in this manner, the psychopharmacology consultant should either change medications or refer to a sub-specialist in affective disorders who can provide the optimal treatment necessary. Finally, the analyst has an ethical responsibility to arrange for continued treatment at a local mental health agency if the patient's funds have run out. To do otherwise is to abandon the patient in the middle of a serious psychiatric episode.

B. CONFIDENTIALITY

Confidentiality is a cornerstone of psychoanalysis, as is privacy. Both are preconditions for the responsible and effective conduct of psychoanalysis and psychoanalytic psychotherapy. Clinical experience repeatedly demonstrates that for patients to speak openly and to approximate free association, they must feel certain that their words will not be disclosed to others.

However, confidentiality is not absolute and it may be breached in a number of situations. These include legal requirements to report abuse of children, intent to harm other people, and other circumstances in which the analyst may be subpoenaed in a legal action. If the analyst is convinced that there is substantial risk of suicide or other self-destructive acts it is ethical to act in order to protect the patient.

It is useful to distinguish between privacy, confidentiality and privilege. Privacy refers to the rights of a patient. Confidentiality is a term that characterizes the ethical and legal requirement for the custodian of health information to not reveal this information except in specific circumstances. A custodian may be a provider of health care or the owner of computerized data. Privilege is a legal term that indicates a special relationship enabling certain individuals to withhold information from a court. This includes the lawyer-client relationship, the spousal relationship and clergy-penitent relationships.

The analyst-patient relationship was not recognized until 1996 when the U. S. Supreme Court established that "reason and experience" lead to the conclusion that protecting the confidentiality of communications between therapist and patient serves both the individual's private interest and the public good by fostering the provision of appropriate treatment. The ruling in the landmark Jaffee v. Redmond case applied only to whether a patient or therapist could be compelled to disclose the content of therapy sessions in the course of a civil proceeding. Lower courts have begun to consider application of privilege in criminal cases but this has not yet been established.

Privacy is the right of the patient, and the analyst may give up confidentiality only with the patient's prior informed consent or in the emergency circumstances listed above. Information that is released may be used only for specific, designated purposes with clear limits and safeguards to prevent further dissemination. The patient has not waived the total right to privacy and confidentiality when signing permission to release information.

When a patient's right to privacy conflicts with needs external to the treatment relationship, such as administrative, research or technical requirements, patient confidentiality and privacy must take precedence. The analyst should use all legal means to safeguard confidentiality.

When a patient wants to use insurance as a means of payment, the analyst should make it clear that there is no guarantee that patients have complete control of access to their records. All information that goes into electronic data banks may be accessed by people who could misuse it. The patient must be aware of this before consent to the release of confidential information can be considered to be informed.

There are other stressful situations for analysts in adhering to the practice of confidentiality. Analysts often hear from patients information about colleagues that may be distressing, and they must compartmentalize what they hear in the clinical setting from other aspects of their lives. Information that is tempting such as financial tips may also be heard and must be similarly protected. It is unethical to use any of this information for personal purposes.

Another common dilemma involves the presentation of clinical material for educational purposes. Every precaution must be taken to protect the patient's identity from being recognized. Some analysts ask current or former patients for permission to use clinical material from their treatment. While this approach has "the advantage of candor" with the patient, it may affect the treatment adversely. Some patients may feel compelled to give or to withhold consent because of the nature of the transference. Even if permission is obtained, however, disguise should be employed.

Analysts can and should feel free to consult a colleague about a difficult case or enlist the aid of a supervisor without feeling that they must mask the identity of the patient if the identifying features are necessary to fully explicate the clinical problem. The patient's permission is not required in order to obtain a consultation. Such consultations are recommended if there is significant uncertainty about what is going on in the clinical situation and may serve, in time, to relieve the considerable burden on the ethical analyst. The consultant is obliged to maintain the patient's and the analyst's confidentiality.

It is also characteristic of analytic practice to be rather isolating and for the analyst to have few opportunities for interaction with colleagues or family and friends about one's daily triumphs or traumas at work. This situation requires that the analyst sacrifice spontaneity in talking with others about patients. It would be unethical to sacrifice confidentiality in order to demonstrate one's mastery of the clinical work. Whereas the patient is free to reveal whatever he or she wishes, including critical, unpleasant or negative distortions, the analyst is not able to express his or her version in rebuttal. The complications that can result from such conflicts can become significant for the analyst. Awareness of and containment of such issues can be a substantial burden to the analyst.

CONFIDENTIALITY / DUTY TO REPORT (B-1-a)

Mr. Frank has been in analysis for 3 1/2 years, initially to deal with his difficult marital relationship and also repetitive episodes of acute anxiety and depressive symptoms for which he has no significant understanding. His analysis has been difficult mainly because he seems highly and chronically resistant to open and genuine free association, and he has been reluctant to indulge in significant regressive fantasy or conscious transference interaction. Dr. Wong has been aware of the patient's resistance and reluctance and has tried gentle interpretation to encourage the patient's capacity for trust and freedom of expression and association. Dr. Wong has noticed that recently there seems to have been a little bit of movement in the direction of openness, trust, and the willingness to confide his inner feelings and experiences.

In this context, Mr. Frank begins to express some of his thoughts and feelings about his adolescent daughter who is now beginning to date boys. She has begun to confide some of her sexual experimentation to Mr. Frank's wife. In the course of this material, Mr. Frank reveals that when his daughter was between the ages of four and seven, he was the parent to supervise her bathing and he was aware that he had washed and manipulated her genital area as part of the bathing ritual. He recognized that this was inappropriate and at the same time felt some sexual arousal. On occasions when Mrs. Frank was away for the weekend, their daughter would come into his bed and sleep in her mother's place.

He was also now aware that as the daughter was going through puberty and developing sexually, that she was provocative and stimulating to him. He found himself fantasizing about her in a sexual way, although he had not made any overt sexual overtures to her.

This new information was expressed with anxiety and shame and at the same time, with a sense of need to confide and understand the nature of his relationship to his daughter. Dr. Wong lives in a state where reporting of sexual abuse of children is mandatory and where the mental health professional who does not report known child abuse, whether occurring currently or in the past, leaves the professional liable to legal prosecution.

What are some of the ethical dimensions of this situation? What should Dr. Wong do, and what are his different options? What would be the likely effects of any of the options that he selects?

CONFIDENTIALITY / DUTY TO REPORT (B-1-b)

Dr. Figueras hears from her patient, Mr. Boyd, that his child is being abused by his wife and that he is distressed by this but does not know what to do. Dr. Figueras is alarmed by this and even feels that Mr. Boyd may be minimizing the situation since he tends towards denial of the many problems in the marriage and family situation.

Dr. Figueras knows that she is legally obliged to report child abuse, but she also doesn't want to do anything that will frighten her patient into fleeing from the analysis. She feels confident that eventually he will see things less defensively and be able to act appropriately on his own, and there is also the very important issue of confidentiality.

But will this possible transformation in her patient be too late to avert a tragedy for the family? To complicate matters she knows how inept the legal system can be in handling such cases. She does not feel that her report will result in prompt and effective action. She doesn't know what the "right" thing is to do, other than to continue to analyze the father of this endangered child. Besides, isn't it possible, although she doubts it, that her patient is misperceiving the situation so that precipitating a report might bring about harm to the wife and disrupt the family as well as the analysis? Is there an ethical dilemma here or only a problem in technique? Are there additional issues and possibilities that Dr. Figueras has not considered? What would be the situation if Mrs. Boyd seriously injures the child? What would Dr. Figueras' situation be if someone else reports the abuse to the legal authorities?

CONFIDENTIALITY / DUTY TO REPORT (B-1-c)

Dr. Johnson is a training analyst who hears from one of his candidate patients during an analytic session that a colleague, Dr. Duval, is becoming demented. Apparently, Dr. Johnson's candidate patient is a close personal friend of another candidate who is being analyzed by Dr. Duval. This friend told the patient that Dr. Duval tells the same joke over and over again, frequently falls asleep during sessions, and calls his patient by the wrong name. Dr. Johnson is deeply troubled by this news but has no other source of information about Dr. Duval's cognitive decline. Dr. Duval attends Education Committee meetings very infrequently and is usually silent during discussions.

Is it enough to hope that other colleagues or supervisees working with Dr. Duval would ultimately bring this to the attention of the appropriate committee or the director of the institute? Whose responsibility is this unpleasant duty? The candidate might expect Dr. Johnson to feel responsibility for taking action, and assume lack of interest if he does not do so. Perhaps he should ask his patient what he is expecting him to do. This would acknowledge the candidate's concerns while helping him clarify his own options and those of his friend. This could be useful analytically. What are some other options?

DISCUSSION

Dr. Johnson is perplexed as to what action he should take. He knows that information he hears from the couch must be kept confidential. However, he is worried that candidates and other patients are being harmed by his inaction concerning Dr. Duval's possible decline. He considers asking his candidate patient to encourage his friend who is in analysis with Dr. Duval to bring this to the attention of the director of the institute or the assistance or ethics committee of the institute. On the other hand, he is uncertain as to the accuracy of the information he is hearing and is equally concerned that pressuring his candidate patient in that way is not in the best interest of the analytic process. He also wonders about setting up a lunch appointment with Dr. Duval so that he could have a personal conversation with him and evaluate his cognitive functioning in that context. But he recognizes that even a lunch appointment such as that would be acting on information he heard from the couch. What should he do?

He is thinking ethically by recognizing that he should not use information obtained from the couch. The Tarasoff decision does not apply here because the harm to patients involved is not in the same category as homicidal threats that might legally require breaching of confidentiality. If he pressures his candidate patient to take action and speak with his friend, Dr. Johnson places both candidates in very difficult positions. He decides to continue analyzing his patient while observing any

*extra-analytic evidence of cognitive decline in Dr. Duval. He
also decides to consult the Analyst Assistance Committee of his
institute to alert them to his concerns without giving the specific information that he has heard from his patient.*

*It is essential to act in association with others to compare
observations and decide on a course of action. It would be unlikely that the transference-influenced patient would be able to
handle the situation without outside help. The profession has a
collective responsibility to safeguard the public and the profession, as well as to care for its own impaired members.*

CONFIDENTIALITY / Patient Protection (B-2-a)

Mr. Albers, a middle-aged professional man, has been in
analysis with Dr. Ostrovsky for the past two years for symptoms
of depression and a feeling of failure in his life. As the analysis
has progressed, Mr. Albers has become increasingly distressed
realizing the difficulties in his own personality, and recognizing
how much he has contributed to his own lack of effectiveness
both in personal and professional relationships. With the depression, he has experienced an increasing sense of hopelessness, feeling that significant improvement in his life and circumstances is
unlikely and that since he has wasted so much of his life he might
just as well die. As his depression has deepened, he has expressed
significant suicidal preoccupation with detailed fantasies of how
he might arrange to complete the act.

Dr. Ostrovsky has become increasingly concerned about
the pressure towards suicide and has recognized the depth of
Mr. Albers's depression. He has suggested the use of antidepressant medication which the patient has refused. He has suggested the possibility of brief hospitalization which the patient
has also refused. Dr. Ostrovsky has also requested permission
to contact Mr. Albers' family and let them know the severity of
the depression and suicidal preoccupation. Mr. Albers indicates
that he does not want his family notified.

Dr. Ostrovsky considers his possible alternatives. Should
he consult with a colleague in order to share the responsibilities for Mr. Albers' suicidal threats? Should he inform the fam-

ily, even though Mr. Albers indicates he does not want this, in order that the family can assist in observing or protecting him? Should he also enlist the family's cooperation so that if Mr. Albers completes the suicidal act he would not be held responsible? Should he discontinue the analysis and refer Mr. Albers to someone else for psychiatric treatment? Should he change the therapeutic focus in his work with Mr. Albers and move to a more supportive psychotherapy situation? Should he deal with his countertransference anxiety by consulting with a colleague but maintain the analytic focus and continue the analytic attempts to work through the suicidal crisis?

DISCUSSION

This case illustrates a variety of conflicting ethical issues. The analyst's obligation first and foremost is to the patient and only secondarily to the patient's family. The principle of confidentiality indicates that telling the family about the suicidal possibility is against the patient's wishes and yet not to tell the family is to place the patient at increased risk of self-inflicted injury.

To discontinue the analysis without the patient's concurrence raises the question of the ethical issue of not abandoning a patient unilaterally. For Dr. Ostrovsky to continue the analysis under the pressure of mounting or sustained anxiety about the patient's ability to control suicidal pressure is to function at less than an optimal level of comfort and may interfere with his judgment. The initial approach should involve a consultation between Dr. Ostrovsky and another experienced practitioner. This may be obtained without the consent of the patient and is not a breach of confidentiality since the consultant is bound to keep the material of the consultation private. The consultation may confirm Dr. Ostrovsky's concern and introduce some new options for dealing with the patient, or the consultant may be reassuring and feel that continuing the analytic work will eventually lead to a successful resolution. In either case Dr. Ostrovsky would obtain the support that he needs in treating this difficult case.

It is not ethical to feel that one must be alone in dealing with exceptional problems. No one person knows everything and it is a sign of mature practitioners that they know when they need help.

CONFIDENTIALITY / Patient Protection (B-2-b)

Dr. Wilson has a patient, Mrs. Young, who recently lost her husband. Since she is both naive and inexperienced in financial matters, it seems to be a good idea for her to consult an advisor to help her manage her assets.

To his dismay, Dr. Wilson hears that she has engaged a Mr. Fox who is known to him as a former patient. Mr. Fox's treatment had been unsuccessful, and he left Dr. Wilson with a substantial unpaid bill. In fact, Dr. Wilson felt that he had been conned into believing that Mr. Fox was always about to receive some money but unfortunately the ship never arrived. At the time that Mr. Fox left treatment, Dr. Wilson was slowly realizing that the man was sociopathic in character.

He would like to protect his patient from the strong probability that she would be similarly conned and yet he is obliged to maintain confidentiality for all patients, both current and former. He is also dealing with his own feelings about this past humiliation and his silence would be self-protective but expose Mrs. Young to a significant financial loss. Lastly, there is the real possibility that if Mrs. Young were to suffer such losses, she would be unable to continue her treatment. She is in a difficult situation which can only be made worse by her contact with Mr. Fox.

What are the ethical issues in this situation? How can the conflict for Dr. Wilson be reconciled? What are the implications for appropriate psychoanalytic technique?

CONFIDENTIALITY / Scientific Issues (B-3-a)

Dr. Chen is preparing a manuscript of a case report describing a very interesting detailed and elaborate account of the analysis of a young man who developed unstable juvenile diabetes during his early adolescence. Throughout the course of the patient's subsequent life history and experience, his diabetic condition varied significantly with his interpersonal relationships. He used the status of his diabetic control, insulin dosage, and diet consciously in his interpersonal relationships, and in his attempts to manipulate or respond to the various conflicts occurring with his biological family. This pattern was repeated in the analytic transference relationship and its management was a significant element of the treatment process. The patient was a psychology graduate student who read the psychoanalytic literature as part of his training.

In an attempt to maintain confidentiality and anonymity of the patient's identity, Dr. Chen disguised the nature of the patient's illness. In order to do so Dr. Chen indicated in the write-up that the illness in question was a peptic ulcer with episodic gastrointestinal bleeding instead of the actual condition of diabetic acidosis or insulin reaction. The paper was eventually accepted for publication in an analytic journal and became a reference citation for the work of other analytic writers and researchers.

Are there ethical issues involved and if so, which ones? Are there scientific issues involved and if so, how do these integrate with the needs for confidentiality and anonymity? Is there conflict between the analyst's wish to publish and the difficulty in fully disguising the case material? Are there other ways of resolving the situation?

CONFIDENTIALITY / Scientific Issues (B-3-b)

Dr. Palmieri has in analysis a fascinating case of a man whose analytic process reveals a great deal of unique and highly significant analytic understanding of early psychic development, For the past year or more, he has been considering the possibility of writing up the case for publication and presentation at a scientific meeting. The patient continues to make progress and the issues that Dr. Palmieri wants to focus upon are becoming even clearer and developed in the patient's material. While not a mental health professional himself, the patient has a great deal of interest in the area and has indicated his desires to read some of the psychoanalytic journals that are currently being published.

Recognizing that the patient might well come upon and recognize even a disguised published report in one of the analytic journals, Dr. Palmieri wishes not to violate the patient's confidences and identity. However, his professional ambitions lead him to wish to publish this material as quickly as possible. The analysis is progressing well and is in its third year, and the patient is significantly immersed in a positive father transference and is deeply appreciative for the analytic progress that he has made to date.

Dr. Palmieri writes the draft of his presentation and shows it to the patient requesting permission to submit it for publication. The patient feels flattered at Dr. Palmieri's interest in publishing an account from his analysis and quickly and readily gives approval to submit the paper for publication.

Is this an ethical or technical problem? Is the patient's consent to publication validly informed and free of transference and countertransference pressures? Are there alternative ways of dealing with this situation? What would be the effect on the analyst and the analysand of the various alternative ways of handling this situation? How can Dr. Palmieri's conflict of interests be resolved?

CONFIDENTIALITY / Legal Testimony (B-4-a)

Mrs. Mirov has been in analysis with Dr. Hansen for the past three years and is recognizing how her masochistic character structure has led her to submit to some of her husband's inappropriate and selfish demands which have caused difficulty and suffering to herself as well as to her children. After much working through, she has come to the realization that it would be in her own best interest to initiate divorce action from the husband and seek custody of the children. Dr. Hansen sees her decision to initiate divorce as a significant step forward in the resolution of her characterological difficulties and feels it to be a sign of increasing self esteem and sense of psychic health.

Mrs. Mirov's husband, however, sees this as an attack on himself and challenges the divorce by initiating a discovery phase by lawyers. Dr. Hansen is called in a deposition to testify about Mrs. Mirov's mental health and her stability in view of her wish to be the custodial parent. Dr. Hansen recognizes that if he is deposed, he will need to violate Mrs. Mirov's confidentiality by discussing his analytic contact with her. Because Mr. Mirov is challenging her mental stability and is using the fact of her analytic treatment as a justification to deny custody, the issue of Mrs. Mirov's mental fitness will probably be seen by the judge as pertinent and Dr. Hansen will be questioned by Mr. Mirov's lawyers.

What are Dr. Hansen's options and what ethical and technical issues are involved? If Dr. Hansen is deposed, should he reveal his position as favoring the divorce, or should he maintain the neutral position he expresses in the analytic sessions? How does the Jaffe vs. Redmond decision by the U.S. Supreme Court impact this situation?

CONFIDENTIALITY / Legal Testimony (B-4-b)

During her treatment and as a result of her improvement, a patient decides to divorce her abusive and litigious husband. They have a child to whom she has been a good and devoted mother. In the state in which they live, the court may examine the psychiatric records of a parent when evaluating his or her fitness to have custody of a child. Her husband threatens to retaliate by waging a custody battle. Although without basis, his attack includes accusing her of being an unfit mother.

The analyst made some notes during the beginning of her treatment. This record contains dreams and fantasies, which if taken out of the context of the analytic situation, could be damaging to the patient. There is also a note about a history of a brief affair at the time of a separation, during which she experimented with marijuana a few times.

The patient indicates that she and her attorney anticipate that the records, if any, will be subpoenaed. They do not know with certainty that any records exist and if records do exist, what is in them. The analyst thinks that it is very likely that the information in the records will be distorted by the husband's attorney and used in a way damaging to the welfare of the patient. The analyst feels caught in a conflict of opposing values. He wants to protect the interests of the patient as well as her confidentiality, but also maintain his professional integrity and legal responsibilities. Although Jaffe v. Redmond may allow the analyst to avoid testifying, his testimony may be needed by the patient to support her child custody hopes.

Should he destroy the records before the anticipated subpoena comes? If the records are subpoenaed, should the analyst release them, refuse to release them, or deny their existence? Should an analyst keep no records if such an outcome is anticipated? Is it unwise to keep detailed records when beginning such a case if there is a likelihood of a possible violation of confidentiality that could occur in the future? Are there other options for the analyst if subpoenaed?

CONFIDENTIALITY / Legal Testimony (B-4-c)

Mr. Carlson has been in four times per week analysis with Dr. Kim for the past three years. During that time, he has worked on the issues of his difficulty in maintaining a strong and committed relationship with anyone, beginning from his adolescence onward and has manifested this by having a series of brief extramarital affairs throughout the duration of his nine-year marriage. His wife feels that he is affectively uninvolved with her, and she has initiated a divorce action in which she sues for custody of their two children.

Mr. Carlson is contesting the divorce and insisting that he has been an adequate husband and provider as well as a devoted father to his children and that Mrs. Carlson has no genuine grounds for her claim to half of his resources. He is prepared to fight for his financial resources as well as the custody issue in regard to his children.

Dr. Kim is aware that Mr. Carlson's attempts to maintain the marriage and to try to retain custody are signs of some degree of maturation as a result of the analytic process and his willingness to commit himself to the relationship. However, the analyst is also aware that if the information about Mr. Carlson's history of marital infidelity and sexual extramarital affairs were to become known to his wife or to her attorneys, it would seriously jeopardize the patient's hopes for himself and his relationship in the marriage. The analyst is also aware that if the divorce procedure moves ahead, he will be deposed in regard to Mr. Carlson's mental state, fitness, character and past history.

Is this an ethical problem or a problem in technique? What should the analyst do in this situation? Should he alert the patient to the possibility of his being deposed? If called, should he reveal the history of extramarital affairs and if so, what effect would this have on the future course of the analysis? Should he conceal that information in any subsequent deposition? There would be a conflict between his required truthfulness in a deposition and his wish to protect the welfare of his patient, and the patient's need for confidentiality. Are there other options for the analyst in this situation?

CONFIDENTIALITY / Educational Setting (B-5-a)

The admissions committee of a psychoanalytic institute routinely circulates a letter to the entire membership requesting information on applicants for psychoanalytic training regarding their qualifications to become a psychoanalyst. The letter states, "Please submit any such information endorsing or opposing the applicant's admission, verbally or in writing," and "All communications will be considered confidential."

A faculty member responded by writing a letter indicating that he had been the mentor for the applicant in question and that the applicant had betrayed him in a dishonest way. The applicant had broken several explicit promises, lied about what he was doing and when confronted, denied responsibility for what had occurred on the grounds that other people were mainly responsible. The applicant had shown neither empathy for those who had suffered on account of the activity, nor was there evidence of any remorse. The analyst concluded that the applicant did not possess the minimal moral character necessary for analytic work. The letter writer further listed several individuals familiar with the situation who would corroborate his statements.

The admissions committee chairperson spoke to the applicant indicating that the applicant's former mentor had written a highly critical letter in regard to issues between them, questioning his moral character and fitness to be an analyst. The chairperson did not actually show the applicant the letter but invited the applicant to write a rebuttal letter.

Faced with contradictory accounts of what had happened in the two letters it received, the admissions committee decided not to seek additional information on the grounds that the committee could not arbitrate the truth or falsehood of the negative claims.

The analyst who had written to oppose the applicant's admission was angry about having been invited to write a confidential letter by a committee that had then violated his confidentiality. He felt the decision avoided the central issue about the applicant's moral character and suitability for analytic work.

How important is an applicant's moral character in assessing suitability? How does an admissions committee assess character and integrity? Assuming reliable evidence of morally reprehensible conduct, is this grounds for denying admission to an analytic institute? Does it make a difference if the misconduct is with colleagues and programs rather than patients?

Is it reasonable to rely on an applicant's training analysis to alter significantly his or her morally dubious behavior? If there is evidence of moral misconduct, what is the responsibility of an admissions committee with respect to protecting future patients? What is the role of admission procedures in maintaining the moral integrity of the field of analysis where character is so important to the work? What is the committee's obligation to maintain confidentiality regarding the solicited letter?

CONFIDENTIALITY / EDUCATIONAL SETTING (B-5-b)

Dr. James is serving as the second case supervisor for Dr. Alden who is an attractive young woman in her early thirties and married to a professor of philosophy. Dr. James had been one of the original interviewers at the time of Dr. Alden's acceptance as a candidate into the institute, and he was generally positive about her potential at that time. The case had started out reasonably well, but as the analysis progressed, there seemed to be an increasing slow-down in the progress and there seemed to be signs that the analyst-candidate was having difficulties understanding and dealing with her patient.

Dr. James recalled from the initial evaluation interviews that the candidate had had some sexual difficulties in her adolescence and also, that there were tensions in her marriage. At times she felt that her husband was remote and not affectively involved with her. Dr. James, calling on the memory of the application interview, suggested to the candidate that she was experiencing sexual countertransference fantasies and wishes towards her analytic patient, and that this probably resulted from the inadequate sexual interaction between the candidate and her husband. Although the candidate was still in her personal analysis, Dr. James further suggested that the patient probably represented a younger brother with whom she had experimented in early adolescence in a sexual way.

Dr. Alden knew that the interpretations could only be based upon Dr. James' recollection of the material she had told him in the application interview, and she protested that these suggestions were inappropriate in her supervision and that they belonged in her personal analysis. Dr. James became annoyed that his interventions were challenged and insisted that her objections to the interventions were a sign of the correctness of his hypotheses. In his next supervisory report, Dr. James reported that Dr. Alden was in difficulty and that she should be placed on academic probation.

What are the ethical problems in using information obtained for one purpose and utilizing it for other purposes? Is this a good educational method? What are some other options?

CONFIDENTIALITY / EDUCATIONAL SETTING (B-5-c)

Ms. Franklin, a third year candidate, is attending a required continuous case conference in which another student is presenting process material. She recognizes that the patient is a neighbor who has confided in her in a personal setting. There are only three students in the class and although she wishes to remove herself, that would significantly change the class dynamic. Also she needs credit for attending this class and she greatly admires and expects to learn a lot from the teacher. If she leaves, she wonders what the other students will think.

What options does Ms. Franklin have and what would be the consequences of them? Is this an ethical issue? Should the Institute administration become involved and if so, how? Can Ms. Franklin listen to the case material and still be able to maintain her previous relationship with her neighbor?

CONFIDENTIALITY / ANALYST'S PERSONAL ISSUES (B-6-a)

A candidate in supervision presented the following ethical dilemma. Her first supervised case had been a man assigned to her through the Institute Clinic and, therefore, the patient was aware from the very beginning of the analysis that she was in supervision. Issues in the situation of supervision had been raised a number of times during the early phases of the analysis and had been dealt with analytically by the candidate in an effective fashion. The analysis was now in its third year and the patient had made rapid progress. The issues of supervision had long since been absent from the analytic dialogue.

After a long phase of erotic and idealized positive transference, the patient had suffered a significant disruption and interference with his fantasies of a final positive ongoing relationship to the analyst. The transference shifted to a negative, disappointed, hurt, angry, and accusatory transference in which the patient experienced the analyst as coldly rejecting. He accused her of making multiple mistakes and of seducing him into the most intense relationship in his life, then coldly and forcefully rejecting him.

The patient arrived for his session carrying a six-page, single spaced letter to the analyst which he gave her with the request that she not share or discuss this with her supervisor. The candidate attempted to discuss this from an analytic perspective with the patient, but he was firm in his reluctance to discuss it beyond the level of his request.

When the candidate came to her next supervisory session she mentioned the existence of the letter but not the content and indicated that she would like to discuss the impact and the content of the letter in supervision but had questions as to whether or not it would be appropriate.

The supervisor indicated directly that she should not discuss the letter or its contents since that would be a breach of the psychoanalytic relationship and whatever the letter's content, the patient's request should prevail. He pointed out that if the letter were to be discussed, the patient's question, "Did you discuss this with your supervisor?" would have a potentially disruptive impact on the entire analysis. If she had discussed it and answered "yes", it would have been a difficult reality for the patient to accept and would further have emphasized his feeling that she was indifferent to him and his wishes. If, on the other hand, she answered, "no" and this was in fact untrue, she would then be in the position of having lied to her patient and this would then create a very difficult interaction in which her secret knowledge of the truth would be disruptive to the analytic listening stance.

The supervisor advised the candidate to attempt again to discuss the patient's request analytically and to raise the question of the supervisor's presence and the implications that it had for him. The candidate concurred in the decision and discussion and left feeling significantly more comfortable and reassured.

What are the ethical issues in this situation? Were there alternative options for the candidate or the supervisor?

CONFIDENTIALITY / Analyst's Personal Issues (B-6-b)

Dr. Hyde has never been particularly interested in financial matters and fortunately for him, his investments have been managed by Uncle Dinero who has proved to be quite competent in this area. When his patients talk of such matters Dr. Hyde has no tendency to be distracted from paying full attention to the analytic process and progress.

However, when Mr. Shekel, an investment banker, began talking about his negotiations with a new company, Dr. Hyde listened even more closely than usual because he recalled vaguely that his uncle had been mentioning this company as a potential new source for a substantial profit. But he chided himself for this lapse and returned his attention quickly to his patient's Oedipal struggles as manifested in the negotiations.

Some weeks later he noted that his patient had withdrawn his bank's support from the company and had detailed to him the corruption and illegality that were sure to put the Amazon Company into bankruptcy. Dr. Hyde dealt with the transference issues but wondered if he should mention to his uncle that he would prefer not to invest in Amazon. While it was not common for him to take active interest in management of his money he had in the past occasionally made some suggestions and he felt that he could casually handle it and thus avoid a loss that would be considerable. He considered the issue of confidentiality but decided that this was not involved since Mr. Shekel's name would never be revealed.

Has Dr. Hyde missed other ethical issues? Should he consider the impact on himself in making a decision to speak or not speak to his uncle? If he withdraws his funds from this precarious situation and it turns out that his patient was wrongly evaluating what was a really valuable opportunity, how might this impact on his ability to retain his analytic stance? If he re-

mains silent and the Amazon situation causes him to suffer
losses, what might be the impact on the analytic situation?
Should he instruct financially savvy patients that he would prefer that they never mention particular company names when
they are on the couch?

CONFIDENTIALITY / Aɴᴀʟʏsᴛ's Pᴇʀsᴏɴᴀʟ Issᴜᴇs (B-6-c)

The patient was a 45-year-old woman who lived in the
same community as the analyst and his family. She repeatedly
tried to make the analytic relationship into a social friendship
both during and after the analysis. Interpretations about this
were rejected during the analysis and impossible after the
analysis was terminated when she moved to another nearby
community.

After the termination she dropped off an expensive gift at
the analyst's home and met his teenage daughter. She invited
the girl to babysit for her. At the country club the ex-patient's
husband offered a good and well paying summer job to the analyst's son who was employed in a menial job at the club.

The analyst was very upset about these intrusions and conflicted about his wish to protect both his family and their privacy and also to protect the ex-patient's privacy and the confidentiality that is an integral part of the analytic process. He
also felt that this patient did not have an adequate termination
and was still narcissistic and would be vulnerable to actions
that she could regard as a rejection.

What is the ethical problem, if any, and what should be
done, if anything? What can be told to the family members
asking about what is going on? What is the analyst's responsibility concerning confidentiality for a former patient?

CONFIDENTIALITY / Aɴᴀʟʏsᴛ's Pᴇʀsᴏɴᴀʟ Issᴜᴇs (B-6-d)

Mr. Bond is the president and CEO of a small technical
corporation and has indicated during the course of his psychoanalytic treatment that he is working on a new process that

may revolutionize the field in which his company functions. Mr. Bond is a self-made man who has usually succeeded in anything he attempts, and judging from the patient's account of the developments, it seems as if this may be a significant breakthrough and result in a major expansion of the patient's corporation

Dr. Singh has a regularly scheduled meeting with his financial advisors during which one of the advisors mentions that there is a rumor that a particular corporation is about to make a breakthrough and that the potential financial profits might be considerable. It turns out that this is the same corporation about which he has been hearing from the couch.

What should Dr. Singh do with this information? Does the principle of confidentiality include information in regard to issues which are already in the public domain?

CONFIDENTIALITY / ANALYST'S PERSONAL ISSUES (B-6-e)

Dr. Diamond is wondering if she could push the rules on confidentiality in the following manner. She has one patient whose husband runs a jewelry business and is in dire need of an experienced stone setter. Another patient, who is currently unemployed, appears to have the precise qualifications that her patient's husband needs for his business. She is tempted to tell the unemployed patient that she heard about a possible job, not involving her patient by name.

Is there any possible down side to passing along this kind of information? Or is this simply a kind act that will help two people and harm no one.

C. AVOIDING EXPLOITATION

Potential for exploitation in the psychoanalytic situation arises in part from the inevitable power differential between patient and analyst. Patients are vulnerable when they come for treatment of neurotic character structure and interpersonal difficulties. Superimposed on this, the procedures of analysis encourage free association and expression of usually suppressed feelings which contribute to major regressive tendencies. There is also the intensity of the transference which is ordinarily much more powerful and insistent than is the analyst's countertransference. All of this places the patient in a position in which he or she can be vulnerable to an exploitative analyst.

The usual rewards of the position and function of the analyst are the fees that are paid as well as the significant professional satisfaction of the work itself. There is pleasure in being involved in an endeavor in which psychological growth is fostered and observed occurring in another person. The analyst is expected to be available to the patient to use as a transference object, and to understand the transference without responding with an emotionally inappropriate countertransference. The analyst will evoke idealizing and other positive, loving transferences, as well as negative, hateful transference feelings. The analyst must have insight and resist the temptation to act on these feelings. Countertransference enactments can be dangerous and destructive to the analytic process and must be monitored. Continuous self observation and restraint from personalized or uncontrolled emotional responses are necessary for the analyst. This sense of monitoring and abstinence can become burdensome, particularly since the analyst is repeatedly exposed to many very intense feelings from each patient.

The fact that the patient's needs and welfare must be primary may even stimulate unconscious transference rivalry, envy and resentment in the analyst, particularly at times when the analyst may be functioning less than optimally. At such times the analyst becomes vulnerable to a variety of affectively charged countertransference responses. This may lead to unconsciously exploitative behaviors which can be rationalized in various ways as beneficial to the patient. When analysts have personal difficulties they may be more likely to use the therapeutic relationship to satisfy their own needs.

Usually boundary violations, as contrasted with boundary crossings, fulfill the transference wishes of analysands, thus stimulating participation in the unethical activity. The regressive transference trust encourages the patient to accept reassurances that all is well and appropriate in the treatment. Boundary violations, whether sexual or nonsexual, are a major threat to the analytic process and to both individuals' emotional health.

Internalization of ethical values that proscribe exploitation in any form guards the best interests of the patient and analyst, as well as students, supervisees and colleagues and the profession in general.

AVOIDING EXPLOITATION / Sexual Boundary Issues (C-1-a)
The Sexual Predator:

Dr. Honig received a call from a 27-year-old single woman requesting a consultation in regard to her psychoanalysis. The patient recounted the following history.

She was a mental health professional who sought consultation with Dr. Maloney, a well known analyst, to understand some of her countertransference reactions to her clients. Dr. Maloney indicated the importance of personal self awareness and suggested that she undertake a personal analysis as a means of enhancing her therapeutic potential for work in this field. He further indicated that he was the best person to see her and that he would be willing to see her at a reduced rate, recognizing her single status and the limitations of her financial situation. She felt flattered, appreciative, and eager to accept his invitation and she began analysis.

After approximately six months of this arrangement, Dr.

Maloney suggested a change in the time schedule and they began meeting late in the afternoon so that she became his last patient of the day. She felt flattered when he began to confide in her regarding some of his marital problems and his lack of intimacy with his wife, and she entertained fantasies of being a better wife to him than was the woman to whom he was married. She was also puzzled that although she was behind in her fee payments, he seemed to accept this without concern and continued to see her, gradually extending the length of their sessions and beginning to voice his appreciation of her listening to his difficulties.

She was unclear as to how it initially occurred, but this evolved into a regular sexual relationship in which during and/or after her formal analytic sessions she would have sexual relations with Dr. Maloney, and frequently he would express his love and interest in her.

However, as time went on, she became aware that her analysis was increasingly secondary to the sexual arrangement and was no longer an ongoing process. She recognized how difficult this relationship was becoming and how it had jeopardized her capacity to relate to some of the men who were asking her out on dates. She felt increasingly burdened, guilty, and anxious and thus initiated the request for a consultation.

Dr. Honig pointed out that her analysis had been irretrievably compromised and that if she expected to gain any kind of therapeutic help, it would be necessary to refer her to a different analyst. He said that her analyst had violated the boundaries of the analytic situation in a form that was impossible to repair and strongly recommended that she discontinue her treatment and all contact with Dr. Maloney.

The patient felt distressed by his recommendation and indicated that she loved her analyst deeply, wished him no harm, and wanted to continue in her treatment with him. She also indicated that she would not bring a complaint against him. Although she could see the rationale to Dr. Honig's recommendations, she felt that she could not follow them. Dr. Honig reiterated his recommendation and indicated that she should consult him again if she changed her mind.

What options does Dr. Honig have? What are his responsibilities to the patient, the profession and the public in this situation? What issues of confidentiality are involved?

Four months later, Dr. Honig received an urgent request for a consultation from the same patient. When she appeared for the session she was tearful, distraught, hurt, and angry. She had been confiding in a friend and found out the friend was also a patient of the same analyst. To her intense dismay, she found that the friend had been experiencing the same kind of sexual contact and verbal expressions of love. She felt betrayed and intensely angry and experienced an acute sense of humiliation and self-hatred for having been "so naive and unthinking." She now indicated that she was willing to initiate an ethics complaint. Dr. Honig arranged to see the patient two more times to help her deal with the acute distress she was experiencing and then was able to refer her to another analyst for definitive psychoanalytic treatment.

Should Dr. Honig have initiated a complaint after the first consultation in spite of the patient's reluctance? What would have been the likely complications for the patient if he had done this? What are Dr. Honig's responsibilities to Dr. Maloney as a colleague? What does this case illustrate in regard to the "slippery slope"?

AVOIDING EXPLOITATION / Sexual Boundary Issues (C-1-b) Countertransference Enactment:

Dr. Amin received a call from a colleague, Dr. Costas, requesting an urgent consultation. He was seeking help in understanding his own actions with a patient.

Dr. Costas had been functioning at his usual level and was enjoying his psychoanalytic practice. As far as he was aware his personal life was smooth, and he was highly satisfied with his marriage and his relationship with his children. However, he found himself having sexual fantasies about a young woman who was experiencing an eroticized transference relationship to him. He was aware of her seductiveness, as well as of her past history of having been sexually abused as a child by a favorite uncle. He was also aware of how this might impact upon his patient's transference experience, and anticipated that she would probably be making significant sexually provocative overtures to him as part of the analysis.

For the first three years of the analysis the process had unfolded effectively, and there was progressive improvement and change in the patient, her behavior, her symptoms, and her sense of self-esteem. He felt a sense of professional pride in his work and in the patient's progress, and he had not been aware of any major disruptive countertransference impulses or fantasies previously.

A week ago he awakened from a sexual dream involving his patient and he noted in subsequent analytic sessions that he was preoccupied with erotic fantasies and realized that for him this was not a usual response even to sexually provocative patients. Two days before the consultation, he had embraced the patient as she arose from the couch and kissed her passionately on the lips as she left the hour.

Badly shaken by his own awareness of the inappropriateness of his behavior and countertransference enactment, Dr. Costas struggled to understand the disturbance within himself. When the patient returned the following day he indicated to her directly that what had occurred the previous day was a response based on his countertransference and that he would need to understand and analyze his behavior, and he hoped it would not disrupt the course of the effective psychoanalytic work that had been done between them.

Dr. Amin recognized that Dr. Costas felt extremely guilty that he had betrayed his analytic role. He seemed not to understand origins or the nature of his countertransference with this particular patient, since this had been an apparently isolated event in his practice. Dr. Costas was also clearly asking for help to cope with the situation.

What options does Dr. Amin have? What are his obligations to the patient and to the profession in regard to Dr. Costas' countertransference and its enactment? What are his obligations to a colleague asking for help?

What about his duty to report violations? Has the analysis conducted by Dr. Costas been irretrievably compromised? Should Dr. Amin suggest that Dr. Costas undergo further personal therapy? Should he suggest that he arrange supervision of his work?

AVOIDING EXPLOITATION / Sexual Boundary Issues (C-1-c) THE "LOVE SICK" ANALYST:

Dr. Sanders, a recently appointed Training Analyst, received a call from a former patient whom he had seen some years earlier in consultation and had referred to a well-respected analyst in the community for treatment. The former patient felt a need to consult with him to discuss events currently occurring in her analysis.

Her analysis had gone extremely well for the first four years of the treatment and she had felt herself increasingly comfortable, confident, creative and she was achieving considerable success in her newly developing career. She had become aware of her analyst making increasingly complimentary comments and wondered why the atmosphere in the analytic sessions felt uncomfortable.

A week before the consultation, her analyst had unexpectedly embraced her as she got up from the couch and had kissed her passionately. He then apologized for his impulsiveness, but in the following analytic sessions he indicated his deep love for her and a feeling that he had fallen in love as never before, and that he wished to discontinue the therapeutic relationship and engage in a personal relationship instead. The patient was thrilled but at the same time frightened at what was occurring, feeling that she had loved her analyst deeply and that they would eventually engage in a marital relationship, while at the same time feeling vaguely uncomfortable and threatened by what had happened.

Dr. Sanders was deeply troubled by the patient's account of what had occurred. The analyst was someone whom he had previously regarded with great admiration and was also someone prominent in the analytic community. On the other hand, he had known that the analyst was recently divorced from his wife and had been observed to be depressed. Dr. Sanders felt a deep distress over his awareness that the analyst had violated the the analytic relationship and while it may have been due to the analyst's depressive situation, it nevertheless constituted a significant boundary issue. The patient did not wish to make a formal complaint against her analyst and requested that Dr. Sanders maintain the confidence of her consultation with him.

What are some of Dr. Sanders' options? Should he initiate an ethics complaint? Should he seek to persuade the patient to initiate an ethics complaint? Should he insist that the patient shift to another analyst? Should he speak to the analyst himself?

Should the Analyst Assistance Committee be notified that the treating analyst may be disabled by depression? How can that be reconciled with the patient's request that the consultation be kept confidential?

DISCUSSION

Dr. Sanders, the consultant for the patient of the love-sick analyst, has a number of complex and difficult ethical dilemmas in front of him. Assuming that the patient's account was accurate, Dr. Sanders learned that the analyst was blindly enacting a series of boundary crossings leading to boundary violations in the form of the passionate kiss followed by the declarations of love. He completely lost his therapeutic role by exploiting the patient's transference feelings in order to gratify his personal urges and wishes. His analyzing capacity was severely impaired by his inability to monitor his own reactions to his recent divorce and subsequent depression.

Dr. Sanders' first obligation is to help the patient by exploring her thoughts and feelings about her analyst's transgressions and to validate the appropriateness of her seeking help. He could help her recognize that both she and her analyst were responding to powerful unconscious forces and that the analytic situation was damaged beyond repair. He could emphasize the disastrous consequences were she to continue a rela-

tionship with Dr. Sanders. He should help her develop options for dealing with the harm that was done to her and assist her in getting into treatment with another analyst who could be reliably ethical. He would need to allow sufficient time for the patient to process her reactions and to deal with his own reactions to his colleague's behavior.

The issue of the patient filing an ethics complaint would have to be viewed in the light of her personal psychological needs as they are revealed in the course of an extended consultation. He should consider whether filing a formal ethics complaint would be clinically useful to the patient and constructive in preventing harm to other patients, as well as persuading the analyst that he urgently needs help in dealing better with his feelings. The consultant also has an obligation to his colleague and to his patients, as well as to the profession and public in general. Although these concerns are substantial, his first concern should be for the patient. That is why she must be made aware of all options, including that of utilizing an appropriate Analyst-Patient Assistance Committee, so that she has an opportunity to express her feelings of exploitation and betrayal and to obtain restitution in some form. If the analyst is uncooperative in this endeavor, this may persuade her to escalate the level of official notification to an Ethics Committee.

The question of confidentiality has to be carefully handled. If the patient wants the complaint to remain confidential, she is making it impossible for either Dr. Sanders or an Assistance Committee to confront her analyst with the entire story. But he might seek her agreement to confront the boundary violation without divulging the specific source of the information and see what would develop from that move. At least the analyst would be put on notice that there is a problem that he has to address. Some feel that Dr. Sanders could break confidentiality in order to notify an Ethics Committee in order to prevent harm to other patients. But the effect of this on the consulting patient would have to be carefully considered.

It would be desirable for Dr. Sanders to try to involve some colleagues in the decision-making process so that his own reactions are validated and processed carefully with due regard for the ethical needs of the profession without forgetting the needs of the patient. It would be a further exploitation to use her situation against her wishes to accomplish other needs than her personal well being. All of the possibilities, implications and options in this highly emotionally charged situation would have to be carefully and tactfully explored with her. If the patient insists on a continuation of complete confidentiality, Dr. Sanders can respect that but still obtain a consultation without using any names. Although this precludes confronting the errant analyst, it may still be useful for Dr. Sanders to validate his work and to help him think of various approaches that may enable the patient to allow herself to make a complaint. In any case, no one should have to deal with such troubling ethical dilemmas alone.

AVOIDING EXPLOITATION / Non-Sexual (C-2-a) Fees:

Dr. Jones is affiliated with an insurance company as a provider which means that she agrees to accept the insurance company rate as full payment for her services. What are the ethical considerations in this arrangement? Should the analyst be concerned with the patient's financial circumstances in dealing with this situation?

DISCUSSION

Accepting or not accepting insurance plans is a personal decision that all practitioners must make. It is ethical to make either choice. If the analyst has decided to accept certain insurance plans the implication is that the insurance fee is at least acceptable, even if less than the analyst would like to get. The patient should be informed that treatment reports may be required to activate the payments and then it becomes the patient's choice to use or not use their insurance to pay for treatment. Patients often do not realize that reports may be disclosed in certain legal situations. Reports should be discrete which means that they tell no more than is necessary, that they

are truthful and that they are discussed with the patient.
Priority must be given to the welfare of the patient and atten-
tion paid to maintenance of the therapeutic alliance.

The patient's financial circumstances should be part of the
total picture. Some patients need to use the insurance to afford
treatment. Others could afford a full fee without insurance but
choose to utilize their coverage.

Attending to the welfare of the patient in a broad sense
means that the feelings of the patient about spending less than
they could afford which gives the analyst a reduced fee must be
handled clinically. On the other side, financially struggling pa-
tients have feelings about getting a reduced, insurance based fee.
The actual wealth or poverty of the patient is just another tech-
nical, clinical factor. The analyst's feelings about the fee and the
patient's financial situation have to be dealt with by the analyst
as a part of ongoing self observation and monitoring. Greed is
not ethical, or healthy either for analyst or patient.

AVOIDING EXPLOITATION / Non Sexual (C-2-a)
Fees:

A child analyst agrees to evaluate a child of a professional
couple in regard to the nature of the child's pathology and the
recommendations for treatment if appropriate. In due course
the child is brought by the parents and, in the second consultative interview, the parents ask the analyst what will be the fee
for the consultation. The analyst's response is that this is an
evaluative series of consultations and that the fee should be discussed after the evaluation. The evaluation continued for several more sessions at which point the analyst recommended intensive treatment for the child.

The analyst then announced what the fee for service would
be; it turned out to be a figure far higher than the parents had
been expecting and was beyond their financial capacities to
maintain. The analyst insisted that this would be the fee for the
entire series of consultative sessions, and the parents experienced a sense of shock and uncertainty at the size of the bill
and whether or not the therapeutic plans were appropriate.

Is this an ethical issue or is it merely a miscommunication? What are the ethical as well as technical issues involved in the presentation and negotiation of the fee for analytic treatment?

AVOIDING EXPLOITATION / Non Sexual (C-2-a)
Fees:

Dr. Nasser has in analysis a 21-year-old man who is just finishing his college education. His father is a well-to-do businessman who agreed to be responsible for the patient's fee. The procedure that has been used is that Dr. Nasser hands the patient a bill for the sessions of each month. The patient is responsible for giving the bill to his father and bringing the check to the analyst prior to the 10th of each month. There have been times in the past when the analysand reports that his father has "forgotten" to write the check and when his father's business trips make delay in payment a not infrequent occurrence. The analysand is distressed by the father's delays in payment but, at the same time, feels reluctant and unable to change the father's patterns of financial interactions.

For the last 3 months, the analysand has indicated his father's refusal to continue paying. The father feels that the analysis is taking too long and should be over by now and that his observation of the analysand indicates to him, the father, that little progress is occurring. The analysand feels that he is significantly changed in his internal experience and relationships and that he is angry but helpless in dealing with the father's position. The analyst is increasingly concerned at the father's demand and at the same time recognizes that the analysand is unable to pay the analytic fees himself and that there are no other sources of payment. The analyst also recognizes that the analysand is increasingly ashamed and reluctant to come for his sessions and is thinking that probably he should follow his father's wishes and terminate the analysis.

What should the analyst do? If Dr. Nasser allows the patient to abandon the analysis at this point, it would negate much of the analytic progress that has occurred up to now, and yet the analysis seems to be in a stalemate at the moment. The analyst cannot indefinitely continue to treat the patient without remuneration, and the father seems adamant in his refusal to continue paying the fees.

If the analyst interrupts the analysis, is he abandoning his patient? If the analyst continues to see the patient without having regular fee payment, is he sacrificing himself in a masochistic way? What are the options for Dr. Nasser? Whose reality issues should prevail: the analysand's need to complete the analysis or the analyst's need for income? Should the analyst consider a consultation?

AVOIDING EXPLOITATION / Non-Sexual (C-2-a)
Fees-Barter:

Dr. Bartlett saw for evaluation a young artist who was depressed and conflicted about relationships. He earned a meager income as a waiter. He had graduated from a well-known art institute with high honors for creativity and had also won prizes for work entered in local and national competitions for young artists. He brought one of his paintings with him to the third diagnostic session, and Dr. Bartlett was positively impressed by the skill and originality shown in the work.

Other historical and psychological findings in the evaluation indicated that the patient had primarily positive indications for analysis as the treatment of choice and he was highly motivated to obtain it. However, the problem of financing his treatment based upon income and lack of other resources was a major difficulty.

Dr. Bartlett decided that the patient would make a suitable analysand and the treatment was appropriate for his problems. Because he felt this individual had great creative promise for the future he made the following proposal: He would accept during the course of the patient's analysis a fee of $5.00 per session for the four weekly appointments. In addition, the analysand would pay his analytic fees by giving Dr. Bartlett one painting every six months as the financial obligation for the analysis. The prospective analysand felt relieved that analysis would be available to him and readily agreed to the terms.

Is this an ethical issue? Does this form of barter for analytic fees constitute undue pressure? If the analysand proves to be recognized subsequently and the paintings offered as fee increase dramatically in value, what would be Dr. Bartlett's ethical situation? Should the patient be referred for a low-cost analysis to one of the analytic clinics in his city? Are there other options in this situation?

AVOIDING EXPLOITATION / (Non-Sexual C-2-b) PHYSICAL CONTACT:

An analysand who had been in treatment for two years experienced, during the course of her session, a deep sense of sadness and hurt accompanied by uncontrollable sobbing and a feeling of hopelessness as part of her recall of a traumatic event from her childhood. This occurred toward the end of the session in question, and she appeared distraught and bedraggled as she prepared to leave the session.

The analyst, experiencing a deep sympathetic impulse and recalling some of his own troubled childhood experiences, put his arm around the patient's shoulder as she got up from the couch, held her briefly and attempted to comfort her distress. The patient then left the office, and the analyst pondered what had occurred.

He recognized a significant impulsive countertransference reaction and enactment and began to consider how to deal with his response. He recognized the sources of his own distress from the past and recognized how the patient's experience had reactivated a repressed affective response in himself.

In the next session, the patient made no reference to the experience of leaving the previous session. Her associations led back to the traumatic and painful memory from the previous session, and she once again experienced deep sadness and distress.

What should the analyst do in this situation? Is this an ethical issue? If so, which sections of the ethics code are pertinent?

Is this a boundary violation? Is this a boundary crossing? What is the difference between a violation of boundaries and the crossing of a boundary?

DISCUSSION

The single incident described above probably represents a boundary crossing in contrast to a boundary violation. The distinction would include whether or not the behavior becomes repetitive and advances further, and whether or not the material is dealt with analytically in subsequent analytic sessions. If the patient doesn't bring it up, the analyst should mention and inquire about the patient's response to the boundary crossing in the previous session and should explore, with the patient, what it meant to her both positively and negatively. It might become the nidus of a boundary violation if it is unexplored in the analysis or if it becomes a repetitive pattern of interaction. In no case should it be ignored and just forgotten about by the analyst or by the patient.

AVOIDING EXPLOITATION / Non-Sexual (C-2-c)
Conflict of Interest:

An analyst places his vacation house with a realtor seeking a tenant for a month during the summer since he plans a trip abroad. An analysand, seeking a rental in that area is offered the house by the realtor.

She brings this coincidence up during the course of her analytic sessions. For the next week she has a variety of fantasies regarding the possibility of sleeping in the analyst's bed and bedroom, of finding out about him and of simultaneously enjoying the summer location. The analyst primarily listens to the patient's associations and interprets the Oedipal transference themes expressed in them.

Meanwhile, the patient's husband contacts the realtor who is handling the transaction and arranges to rent the cottage for the month at the given price. The realtor draws up a contract and takes it to the analyst, who signs the contract.

The patient, her husband and family rent the cottage for the stipulated month. The analyst has some hesitation in doing this but anticipates that this is all "grist for the mill" and feels that he will be able to deal with this in the analysis. He is concerned about confidentiality, feeling that if he refuses this rental the realtor will guess that this is a patient.

What are some of the ethical issues involved in this situation? Is there a conflict of interest for the analyst or for the patient, or both? Is this a boundary crossing or a boundary violation? Does the analyst have other options and what would be their possible consequences?

AVOIDING EXPLOITATION / NON-SEXUAL (C-2-d)
DUAL RELATIONSHIPS:

One of Dr. Garnier's hobbies is African art, and he has become quite an expert. He has an extensive collection of artwork which is well known in his community. He receives a letter from the local art museum, inviting him to join as a member of the board, to help in the evaluation of the collection and in advising the museum staff on subsequent museum acquisitions. Dr. Garnier is very pleased and promptly accepts the invitation.

At the board meeting he is surprised to see that his analysand, Mr. Kelly, is also a board member. Mr. Kelly had not previously been aware of the invitation tendered to Dr. Garnier. Mr. Kelly's interest in the arts is predominantly focused around late 19th century European paintings.

This situation represents a dual relationship between Mr. Kelly and Dr. Garnier, as they will inevitably have interactions at the various board meetings as well as potential differences of opinion as to how the resources of the museum should be used. Dr. Garnier recognizes the dual nature of the relationship but is also extremely pleased to have been asked to serve on the board and is reluctant to sacrifice his interest in African art and its recognition for the sake of maintaining the purity of the analytic relationship.

Is this an ethical issue? What is the implication of this dual relationship for the subsequent analytic process? Is this different from the situation of training analyst with candidate analysand who may both work on institute committees?

AVOIDING EXPLOITATION / NON-SEXUAL(C-2-d)
DUAL RELATIONSHIPS:

Dr. Gates is the full time Director of Residency at a psychiatric training program at the medical school. He is conducting the analysis of a second year medical student whose treatment has been going well and who is increasingly expressing an interest in the field of psychiatry.

The analysand decides in his senior year to enter psychiatry as a profession and applies to a number of psychiatric training programs including the one in which his analyst is the Residency Director.

Dr. Gates is aware of the many difficulties that might occur in the dual relationship and thus excuses himself from any of the interviewing and residency judging functions related to his patient. However, the department faculty are aware of the analysand's potential in the field and vote to accept him as a resident. The analysand chooses them in the matching program.

The analysand is accepted and plans to join the residency in psychiatry, and Dr. Gates is aware that given the nature of his medical school position, he will be involved in multiple dual relationships with the analysand during the course of his residency.

Is this an ethical problem? What options does Dr. Gates have? Should he interfere with the analysand's professional choices? Should he recuse himself from any considerations regarding the analysand and the residency's educational program? How does he explain this to his staff if he does?

AVOIDING EXPLOITATION / Non-Sexual (C-2-e) Gifts:

Dr. Nakamura is an officer in a moderately-sized psycho-analytic study group which is struggling financially and dissipating its resources. He is also president of the local psychoanalytic foundation, which is now being organized to help support psychoanalysis in the community.

Mr. Raymond, a very personable and intellectually gifted man, has been in analysis with Dr. Nakamura for several years. The analysis has been extremely successful. As a result of their work together, Mr. Raymond has overcome severe internal conflicts that had been standing in the way of his success in his field and the monetary rewards that go with it. He is now wealthy. He has worked through his sexual anxieties and is now happily married to a very appropriate woman from a prominent family. She is also wealthy and has had a successful analysis with one of Dr. Nakamura's colleagues.

Mr. Raymond is now in the termination phase. In his analysis he has been talking about how psychoanalysis has changed his and his wife's lives. He and Mrs. Raymond are genuinely grateful. He says he has heard about the new foundation that is being organized and that they will be enthusiastic supporters. They would like to make a large donation, if they can get information on how to do so.

Dr. Nakamura knows that because of their prominent standing in the community, their financial and public support would be very helpful to the development of the foundation. Mr. Raymond, who is a very good analytic patient, is wondering what his motivations are in regard to his analysis and his analyst. He is actively working analytically on these issues.

What should Dr. Nakamura do in this situation? What are the ethical issues?

AVOIDING EXPLOITATION / Non-Sexual (C-2-e)
Gifts:

Dr. Pappas has been conducting the analysis of a very wealthy financier for whom the analysis has been profoundly meaningful and allowed him for the first time in his life to experience genuine fulfillment and pleasure in his various activities. He is deeply grateful to his analyst and indicates that he wishes to demonstrate his gratitude by donating a significant sum of money for analytic scholarships in the Clinic of the institute to which Dr. Pappas belongs. It is his genuine wish that since he has benefited so extensively from his analysis, less affluent people be offered the same opportunity for help.

The analysis is now in its termination phase and Dr. Pappas questions the motivation behind the analysand's wish to donate the money. After extensive analytic scrutiny, they both agree that the donation is a reflection of the analysand's progress. Dr. Pappas then agrees to the planned donation and indicates to the analysand how and to whom the donation should be made.

Is this an ethical violation? If it is a violation, what issues does the donation raise? If it is not a violation, what issues does the donation raise? When, if ever, would such a donation be appropriate? What limitations, if any, does it impose on Dr. Pappas?

AVOIDING EXPLOITATION / Non-Sexual (C-2-f)
Solicitation of Patients:

Dr. Foster received a call from a 27-year-old single woman requesting a consultation in regard to her ongoing psychoanalysis. The patient recounted the following history.

She had been a student in a psychotherapy program offered by the local psychoanalytic society as part of its community outreach program. Part of the program was that she and one other student shared supervision with an analyst, meeting on a weekly basis.

During the course of her supervision she became aware of

some personal countertransference responses to her patient which she felt uncomfortable in revealing to her fellow student and she therefore requested an individual session with the supervisor. The supervisor, listening to her account of her feelings, indicated the importance of personal self-awareness and suggested that she undertake a personal analysis as a means of enhancing her therapeutic potential for work in this field. He further indicated that he was the best person in the community to see her and that he would see her at a reduced rate.

She felt flattered, appreciative, and eager to accept his invitation and while continuing the supervisory relationship, she began a personal analysis.

But it has become uncomfortable for her to see this person in these dual roles and she wonders if the treatment is such a bargain after all. She feels that she really cannot tell him about this and now she feels trapped, guilty and somehow ungrateful. She sometimes thinks that the only way out is to leave her profession.

Is this an ethical issue or one of pedagogy? What are the options for Dr. Foster? Were there other ways that the supervisor could have dealt with the situation?

AVOIDING EXPLOITATION / Non-Sexual (C-2-g)
Abandonment of Patients:

A mental health professional was in psychoanalytic psychotherapy with an analyst for two years. She had sought treatment following the departure to Europe of one of her oldest friends. She complained of panic, feelings of loss, abandonment and depression. She had a history of maternal neglect with prolonged physical absences and an alcoholic father who had episodes of mania and violence. Despite this traumatic and depriving background, the patient achieved some successes in life. She had a satisfying career in mental health, a strong marriage, and several long-term friendships. She was also a successful painter.

The treatment was helpful, although the patient was critical of the analyst's frequent silences which he ultimately justified by citing his classical theoretical stance. She had originally entered treatment articulating her belief that he was a self-psychologist, a view which he did not question for many months.

Recently her mother died and when she discovered that she had been disinherited, she became very upset. The analyst was somewhat more supportive during this period. At this time the patient brought in some recent paintings for the analyst to see. She felt that the paintings might shed some light on her current state of mind. The analyst made no comment about the paintings other than to note that they represented her resistance to doing the analytic work.

One day she arrived for her appointment and was informed by the analyst that he had a medical emergency in his family and therefore the appointment was cancelled. At her next scheduled hour, the analyst abruptly informed her that he no longer could be as supportive as he had been and that he felt they should terminate.

The patient begged him to allow her to continue, even if he would no longer be especially supportive. He refused and said it could never work out well. The patient asked the analyst whether they should get a consultation, but the analyst refused, saying that he did not think it was necessary. The analyst did say that the reasons for ending had to do with his limitations, but could not express what those were or why they had come up in the context of her current struggles. She asked for a referral, and he said that they could talk about it, but he felt that she could handle this on her own.

At her next appointment, she informed him that she had found another analyst. He was pleased with her choice. This was the final hour. The abrupt ending was very painful.

The patient was diagnosed as having a peptic ulcer two months after the termination.

The patient was very grateful to have found a new analyst who was more openly warm, supportive, and interactive. She was relieved to find that it was not her fault that the earlier analysis had not been successful. In fact, it had been a re-traumatization. She was concerned as a mental health professional that other patients might be similarly hurt by her former analyst who was well-known and respected, but could be so hurtful and non-empathic at times. She wondered what could be done. She was concerned about complaining lest she be dismissed as a problem patient.

Is this abandonment according to our ethics code? What other ways might this analyst have pursued in this situation, either to prepare his patient for the termination or to consider the possibility of countertransference interference? Is this a case for a Colleague and Patient Assistance Committee referral for consultation and/or mediation?

DISCUSSION

This patient felt abandoned by her analyst. She was very upset by the abruptness of the analyst's action and his unwillingness to continue working with her, even in a less supportive mode. The patient felt that she was caught up in some family problems of the analyst.

Technically, the analyst did not fully abandon his patient according to our code, since he offered to continue seeing the patient until she found a new therapist. The patient reported that he was half-hearted in offering to see her until a new therapist was found. However, he was obligated to help his patient find a new therapist which he did not do. While the patient and analyst may have been somewhat mismatched from the onset, nonetheless they seemed to have made some progress. A consultation for the analyst requested by the patient might have restored a more effective, congenial working relationship and prevented the traumatic sudden ending of the treatment which in effect, due to the patient having been disinherited by her mother, constituted a retraumatization.

Consultation for such clinical situations is strongly recommended in our new code. It is conceivable that continuing consultation and/or further analysis for the analyst might have saved the treatment.

Finally, if indeed the analyst could no longer tolerate the alleged neediness of his patient, he might have handled the end-

ing in a less punitive manner. He might even have announced to the patient that at the present time he was not able to provide the kind of treatment that she needed, but that many other analysts could. Thus, the patient could be partially spared the pain of feeling that she was terminated because she was not suitable for analytic treatment. A less abrupt termination would also have been less traumatic.

AVOIDING EXPLOITATION / NON-SEXUAL (C-2-g)
ABANDONMENT OF PATIENTS:

Dr. Townsend was maintaining a full analytic and psychotherapeutic practice but was increasingly concerned about his health, his future and the limited opportunities to spend more time with his family. He and his wife had been speaking about possible retirement plans and locations, and both had a wish to move to an area closer to their children and grandchildren.

On a recent visit to his physician, Dr. Townsend was told that there had been some significant, but as yet asymptomatic, changes in his electrocardiogram suggesting that he may have suffered a heart attack without being consciously aware of it.

This news precipitated a decision by Dr. Townsend and his wife that he should retire, and they used the news about the heart attack as a signal to initiate their plans immediately.

During the next week Dr. Townsend announced to each of his patients that the current session would be the last, that he was retiring from practice, and that they should make arrangements to find another analyst or therapist. Most of the patients were taken by surprise and felt unsure of what to do next. Dr. Townsend suggested that if they needed to, they should consult with other psychiatrists or psychoanalysts in the community for future planning. At the end of the session for each patient, he said goodbye and wished the patient well.

DISCUSSION

The analyst in practice is frequently confronted with a conflict of interest between the needs of his patients and his own personal needs and wishes. There may be occasions when such concerns in the analyst's life override his or her responsibility to the patient (i.e. sudden death and/or life-threatening illness, major disabling accident or trauma, etc). However, in more ordinary situations the code states that "the psychoanalyst should not unilaterally discontinue treating a patient without adequate notification to the patient and an offer of referral for further treatment".

Dr. Townsend's situation had previously been considered by him and his wife. The change in status, therefore, did not constitute a sudden or unexpected or unavoidable event. He could therefore have allowed sufficient advance time to inform patients appropriately. It was, therefore, inappropriate for him to discontinue treatment of his patients without previous notification and opportunity to deal with the patients' inevitable responses to the sudden termination of their treatment. He also did not assist the patients in seeking further evaluation and/or treatment, and in these situations his behavior toward the patients constituted abandonment of them.

It has frequently been recommended that psychoanalysts maintain a current and up-to-date "psychoanalytic will" indicating recommendations for referral to someone else in the event of sudden incapacity or unexpected death of the analyst. A trusted colleague or spouse should be aware of the location of the will in the event of sudden inability to continue practice. The tendency toward denial of mortality leads most analysts to neglect doing this, or if they do make arrangements, not to keep them up to date.

Countertransference factors may have influenced Dr. Townsend's decisions in this situation, but the analyst is expected to at least recognize this possibility and to take appropriate steps to counteract these factors.

AVOIDING EXPLOITATION / NON-SEXUAL (C-2-g)
ABANDONMENT OF PATIENTS:

Dr. Silver has been treating a patient who is paying a regular fee. The patient has heard that layoffs are expected in his company and he expects to be unemployed for some time because the job market will be flooded with people with his qualifications. Is there an ethical obligation to the patient in this instance? What about the analyst's need to take care of himself and his own finances?

D. Relationships with Colleagues, Students, and Supervisees

The relationships with colleagues, students and supervisees should be based on mutual respect and professional acknowledgement. It is likely, however, that these relationships will be influenced by conscious and unconscious factors such as competition, status, reputation and even differences in clinical or theoretical orientation. Where there are biases, either positive or negative, the ethical analyst is expected to recognize them and try to offset them by efforts to be as fair as possible. If this cannot be accomplished, it would be desirable for the biased person not to participate in situations or decisions that could affect another person's professional progress, status or reputation.

Psychoanalysts should avoid deliberately participating in cliques or in attempts to build a following among colleagues. Gossip should also be avoided and an attitude of self-observation should be cultivated so that prejudicial statements and actions may be controlled.

A high level of self awareness in regard to bias and discrimination will enable the psychoanalyst to treat patients, colleagues, students and supervisees with fairness and respect.

RELATIONSHIPS / Professional /(D-1-a)

Dr. Carver, a second year candidate, asked to be supervised by Dr. Friend on his second case. Dr. Friend agreed and supervision began. However, during supervision, Dr. Friend appeared to be less than enthusiastic about the case and repetitively expressed dire and negative opinions about the patient and the patient's ultimate analyzability. He also was critical of Dr. Carver's psychoanalytic technique and felt that he was being influenced by a countertransference response to feel too optimistic and too invested in the analysand.

After about six months, Dr. Carver, in keeping with the institute policy, requested a change of supervisors. His request was approved, and he selected Dr. Ruiz as his new supervisor. Dr. Ruiz hears the case and feels that the patient is analyzable and that Dr. Carver is doing well, although it is a difficult case. Meanwhile Dr. Friend writes a report of his supervisory experience to the institute Progression Committee indicating his negative opinion of Dr. Carver and of the patient and strongly stating that, in his opinion, this case should not be continued nor should it count as one of Dr. Carver's training cases. At the time of the required annual report, Dr. Ruiz submits an essentially positive report on Dr. Carver indicating that although the patient is difficult, Dr. Carver is making solid analytic progress and that he expects the case ultimately to achieve a planned and appropriate termination.

In the Progression Committee meeting, Dr. Friend continues to express his strong negative prognosis and opinion, insisting that he is more objective than Dr. Ruiz and expressing his theoretical differences and criticism of Dr. Ruiz's concepts of psychoanalytic technique. The Chair of the Progression Committee notes the sharp difference of opinion between the two supervisors and senses that Dr. Friend and Dr. Ruiz are using the candidate's situation to express some of their own personal competition and animosity toward one another.

Is this an ethical problem? If it is, what principles are implicated? If not, what is the educational question? What options do the candidate and the committee have in order to achieve a fair resolution?

RELATIONSHIPS / PROFESSIONAL (D-1-b)

A candidate called Dr. Aristide, her Institute advisor, to discuss changing supervisors. She had been presenting a case to

Dr. Singer for some time. The case and her supervision were not going well. Dr. Singer had a reputation as a good teacher and was well regarded by the faculty.

She told Dr. Aristide that she had lost confidence in her work, and perhaps the problem was that she was just not good analyst material. But she was confused because she had another case in supervision with Dr. Miller that had been going well. She reluctantly revealed that, although she thought she might be too sensitive, she felt that Dr. Singer had criticized her with unnecessary harshness and sarcasm and had ridiculed her at times, laughing at her ideas. She said he told her that her work was inadequate; he had made very personal comments to her about her psychodynamics that she felt were intrusive and belonged in her analysis and had become angry and offended if she did not promptly make the specific interpretations to her patient that he had suggested in supervision. She feared Dr. Singer's comments were justified as a consequence of her inadequacy.

Dr. Aristide was concerned that the candidate might have been treated abusively by Dr. Singer but also wondered if the candidate might be displacing transference from her analyst to Dr. Singer. Dr. Aristide suggested that she bring the matter up in her analysis, and then he would like to talk about it with her further. He remembered that in faculty discussions of the candidate, Dr. Singer was mildly critical of her work in certain areas, but not highly so. Reports and discussions concerning her other case with Dr. Miller were positive.

After discussing the matter in her analysis, she brought up the issue with her fellow candidates. She found that two other candidates who were in supervision with Dr. Singer revealed similar experiences. She then reported this information to Dr. Aristide at their next meeting.

Is this an ethical issue? Is it a variant in teaching technique?

What are Dr. Aristide's options? What are the Institute's responsibilities? What are the candidate's options?

RELATIONSHIPS / PROFESSIONAL (D-1-c)

A candidate was serving as candidate representative to one of his analytic society's committees. Listening to members of the committee express various opinions about his analyst, he had many mixed feelings. He associated to these feelings on the couch and was distressed to hear his analyst react with outrage. The analyst later told the candidate that he had called the committee chair to protest.

The candidate felt mortified. He thought he had wounded his analyst and feared both he and the analyst would lose the respect of the committee members. Stating his first loyalty would always be to his analyst, he imagined he might never find a place in the analytic community. He was nervous about even sharing this dilemma outside the analysis.

Is this an ethical problem? Is it an issue of countertransference interference in psychoanalytic technique?

What are some of the institutional and interpersonal issues raised by this situation?

If it involves ethical issues, which parts of the ethics code are pertinent?

RELATIONSHIPS / PROFESSIONAL (D-1-d)

Dr. Aaron, a training analyst, is asked to serve on an institute committee of training analysts that will examine a candidate for graduation through discussion of the case reports that the candidate has submitted to the Education Committee. Some years earlier Dr. Aaron had been the analyst for the candidate's wife and thus through her had heard a great deal about her husband and some of his background. Dr. Aaron remembered that the candidate had suffered the loss of a close family member through suicide when he was a young adult, and Dr. Aaron was searching the case material presented by the candidate for references to possible suicidal thoughts in the patient the candidate was presenting.

During the course of the examination, he asked a number of questions in regard to the patient's possible depressive state and the risk of suicide, asking whether or not the candidate had shown proper concern for this potential event. The candidate indicated that it had not been a significant issue in his patient's material but Dr. Aaron questioned him further as to whether he might have overlooked the potential for suicide in the patient. The candidate was aware of the source of Dr. Aaron's questions and felt somewhat exposed, flustered and defensive but maintained his position. The other members of the committee sensed something unnamed occurring between the candidate and Dr. Aaron but had no awareness of the issues in question.

Is this behavior by Dr. Aaron an ethical violation? If so, what ethical principles are involved?

Should a teacher be free to use information from an analytic patient to deal with the educational issues in a candidate?

Does this situation represent a conflict of interest for Dr. Aaron? Should Dr. Aaron have recused himself because of a potential conflict of interest?

RELATIONSHIPS / PROFESSIONAL (D-1-e)

Dr. Anthony is a training analyst at a Psychoanalytic Institute and has in analysis a recently graduated member of that Institute. The analysand has been in treatment for two years and is experiencing a generally positive analytic process in which the issues previously not fully resolved in his official training analysis are now being dealt with more openly and appropriately. Recently he has been deeply concerned with the difficulties of starting an analytic practice and wonders if he is doing something to interfere with faculty members referring him patients for analysis. Dr. Anthony thinks highly of the analysand's capacities to function professionally and hopes for the analysand's sake that his practice begins to grow.

Dr. Anthony receives a call from a colleague in another city asking him to refer for analysis a young businessman who is moving to Dr. Anthony's location. He wants to refer this patient to his current analysand in hopes that it will reassure the analysand that he has made a good career choice in becoming a psychoanalyst.

Does this reflect a dual relationship between Dr. Anthony and his analysand? What possible effects could such a referral exert on the subsequent analytic process? Is this an ethical issue or is it an issue of psychoanalytic technique? Does it represent a boundary crossing or a violation? What would you do in this situation?

RELATIONSHIPS / Professional (D-1-f)

Dr. Seth Abrams, a Jewish candidate, presented an analytic case of an adult African-American female patient to his Jewish supervisor, Dr. David Stein.

Six months into the supervision, Dr. Abrams thought that the work was going very well. He found Dr. Stein to be keenly interested in the patient's psychodynamics, her evolving erotic transference reactions to Dr. Abrams, and the interplay between her intrapsychic conflicts and the traumas of her early life. These included abject poverty and two years of separation from her mother from ages one to three. As the patient began to resist actualization of her erotic transference wishes for the analyst, she became intensely focused on her need for the analyst to be a consistently nurturing mother and her fear increased that he would eventually abandon her. She then became preoccupied with her disappointment that her analyst was not African-American.

Dr. Abrams continued to feel helped by Dr. Stein, although the candidate was quite anxious about how to address the patient's concretizations of race. Dr. Stein was very skillful in helping Dr. Abrams track the defensive aspects of the patient's reactions and in helping him to work with the patient on the transference displacements to race. They were successful in helping themselves and the patient to gain a fuller understanding of the various meanings packed in the patient's uses of race without the patient becoming too threatened and thus even more defensive.

However, in a series of sessions following the analyst's unexpected week-long absence due to illness in his family, the patient began to express rage over the fact that millions of slaves had been killed in transit from Africa to America. She began to express grave disappointment and rage that America had never come to terms with this atrocity. Though she did not explicitly mention her analyst's Jewishness, she expressed doubt that he could understand how she felt. At this point, Dr. Abrams was stunned when his supervisor erupted in a lengthy discourse on the fate of the Jews in the Holocaust and how there was no reasonable comparison to be made between the fate of the Jews and the fate of African slaves. Dr. Abrams was so unsettled by this departure from the supervisor's usual close attention to analytic process and by his own view that the supervisor was off track that he could not make any use of that supervisory hour.

When Dr. Abrams consulted another supervisor about his feeling that Dr. Stein had lost it and was perhaps demonstrating prejudice or insensitivity, Dr. Abrams was advised that Dr. Stein's narcissism would not allow him to meaningfully discuss what had happened. He was told that it would not be a good idea to try to talk to his supervisor about what happened. Dr. Abrams did not question this opinion or seek other advice. Thereafter, Dr. Abrams felt the supervision was stunted and not useful, and he discontinued as soon as he reached the minimum number of required hours.

DISCUSSION

What does Dr. Stein's racial and cultural insensitivity represent? Was he overwhelmed momentarily by emotional issues related to his own ethnic identification or is he demonstrating a deeply ingrained racial prejudice? Did he show a lapse in competence? Did he demonstrate a lack of respect and care for the racial identity and issues of the patient? Could the situation have been corrected by Dr. Abrams trying to bring him back on the usual supervisory track? Why might Dr. Abrams not have tried this approach?

How might we understand the second supervisor's advice to ignore what had happened? Was the second supervisor meeting the Institute's obligation in this circumstance? Was he taking an opportunity to express some personal animus towards Dr. Stein?

How can we understand Dr. Abrams' uncritical willingness to accept this second supervisor's opinion and to give up what had been a productive relationship for several months. How was Dr. Abrams' work and psychoanalytic development hurt by what happened?

What is an Institute's responsibility in such a situation, and what are other options for a supervisee who is troubled by the actions of a supervisor?

RELATIONSHIPS / PROFESSIONAL (D-1-g)

Dr. Okuno had conducted the application interview of a 31-year-old woman applying for psychoanalytic training at his institute. During the course of the interview, he found out that she had been married for three years and that she and her husband were attempting to achieve a pregnancy in order to start a family. She indicated that she hoped to have several children and that this was an important and emotionally significant issue for herself. She also indicated that she wanted to begin her analytic career as quickly as possible and that she had always worked hard in her academic programs.

In his written report, Dr. Okuno indicated that the applicant was probably acceptable as an analytic candidate, but he recommended that she be deferred for admission. He based his recommendation on the fact that she was intent on becoming pregnant as soon as possible, and that if she were to become pregnant, it would conflict with her wishes for analytic training. It was his opinion that she would be intensely invested and involved in the pregnancy, given the importance that it had for her, and that there would probably be several other pregnancies and that during those times it would be inappropriate for her to invest the necessary amount of energy and emotion in her training. It was also his opinion that the first year or two of an infant's life was crucial for future development and that mothers should remain at home taking care of their children during that time. Therefore, he felt that it would be inappropriate for this applicant to engage in a new career while trying to raise small children.

In the Admissions Committee meeting, Dr. Okuno maintained the same positions and voted to defer the applicant's admission until such time as her children were old enough to enter nursery school or day care. He reiterated his belief that a mother of small children must give her primary emotional involvement to the children and that the initiation of a new career would jeopardize that involvement.

Is this an ethical question? If so, which portions of the Ethics Code are involved? Is this an example of personal bias? If so, how should Dr. Okuno's opinion be considered? How should the other members of the Admissions Committee handle this situation?

RELATIONSHIPS / PROFESSIONAL (D-1-h)

During the course of an analytic session, a candidate in analysis with Dr. Higgins describes how Dr. George, during a class teaching session on psychoanalytic technique, has publicly stated that most of the faculty in the institute know very little about psychoanalysis or the psychoanalytic process. The candidate goes on to indicate that during a social hour reception at a recent psychoanalytic society meeting, Dr. George had expressed sharply contemptuous opinions in regard to several specific members of the Society and their techniques of psychoanalytic treatment. Dr. Higgins wonders as he listens whether there are transference meanings for the analysand in these associations, but does not actively intervene.

At a subsequent psychoanalytic meeting in another city, Dr. Higgins meets an old friend, Dr. Smith, and they have a drink together. Dr. Smith indicates his understanding that the psychoanalytic situation in Dr. Higgins' home city is desperate, and that there are rumors to the effect that the Institute should be disaccredited. When asked where his information came from, Dr. Smith indicates that Dr. George has been speaking to a number of people around the country about his perceptions of the situation, and that a good deal of negative gossip is now occurring.

Dr. Higgins recognizes that this information is in keeping with the reports that he had heard from his candidate analysand and that considerable damage is being inflicted on the individuals and the group of analysts in his Institute and Society.

What, if anything, should Dr. Higgins do? Dr. George's behavior as indicated from the candidate's analysis is apparently being confirmed by Dr. Smith in a social context.

DISCUSSION

Dr. Higgins correctly recognizes that the report from the candidate's analysis is covered by issues of confidentiality and is not to be used to deal with the situation in regard to Dr. George. However, it does serve to alert Dr. Higgins to the fact that there may well be some type of damaging behavior going on. He is aware that some of the faculty members in the Institute have had somewhat negative and difficult relationships with Dr. George. He has been aware, as have other members of the Society, that Dr. George tends to be a "loner" and has few close contacts in the psychoanalytic community. Dr. George is a training and supervising analyst and, as such, has significant impact on a variety of analysands and supervisees, as well as on the group involved in classroom teaching. He recognizes that the situation may become damaging to the analytic community if left unchecked.

At the same time, however, he is aware that the needs for confidentiality of the analysand preclude him from mentioning that source and that the information from Dr. Smith is "hearsay" and possibly somewhat distorted. He is aware that it is unlikely that Dr. Smith has a personal motivation for revealing the information, and it is probably a function of Dr. Smith's friendship with Dr. Higgins.

It seems to Dr. Higgins that Dr. George is deliberately ex-

pressing prejudicial statements and actions and that although he may firmly disagree in regard to a difference of opinion in connection with psychoanalytic technique, he nevertheless is expressing a personal attack that is doing damage to the other psychoanalysts in his community.

One possible alternative would be to share the conversation he had with Dr. Smith with the executives of the Institute and/or Society so that the burden of decision making is shared with others. This would not violate the confidentiality of his analysand and therefore would be acceptable in the context of protecting the Institute and his colleagues against the effects of Dr. George's remarks to the general psychoanalytic community. It would seem that Dr. George's behavior is not in keeping with the ethical principle of personal integrity that "the psychoanalyst should be thoughtful, considerate, and fair in all professional relationships, uphold the dignity and honor of the profession, and accept its self-imposed disciplines. He or she should accord members of allied professions the respect due their competence."

Dr. Higgins might initiate an ethics complaint with the officers of the Institute, requesting a preliminary investigation which might then allow an open discussion of Dr. George's behavior and its effects in the local and general analytic communities. Knowing that analytic candidates are deeply influenced by their training analysts and their supervisors and also knowing that the status of a training analyst is a privilege and not a right, Dr. Higgins might also consider bringing up the question of whether Dr. George's status of training analyst should be continued or whether he should be removed as a training and supervising analyst.

This is a deeply felt and distressing situation; such situations promote confusion and difficulty among the candidates of an institute and also damage the ongoing, comfortable, collegial relationship that is optimal for educational purposes. Differences of opinion must be recognized and encouraged but in an atmosphere that is free, as much as is possible, from bias or personal critical and contemptuous attack.

RELATIONSHIPS / PROFESSIONAL (D-1-i)

Dr. Green, a training and supervising analyst who is widely respected in the community, has been nominated to become the president of the local psychoanalytic society at the next election. Anticipating the small turnout that usually exists as part of the election process, Dr. Green is attempting to encourage colleagues and younger students and analysands to vote for him in the election. He emphasizes that he would be grateful for the support of his supervisees and analysands and indicates to them in direct, as well as indirect, ways that analytic referrals might come their way if he were to be elected president. He also encourages some of his supervisees to speak positively about him and show their support among colleagues and others in the analytic community.

An analytic candidate in analysis with you reveals during several analytic sessions the pressure he feels from Dr. Green to support his election as president of the Society. He feels torn between his loyalty and wish to support someone who offers potential for analytic referrals as opposed to his discomfort at having Dr. Green so strongly and repeatedly attempting to influence his vote. At one session, he reports that a number of candidates in a semi-social situation expressed concerns similar to his own in regard to Dr. Green's seeking to develop a clique of younger colleagues who would support him and his position.

The problem of confidentiality of an analysand's communications make it unethical to use the information regarding Dr. Green obtained from the analysand as the basis for any type of action. On the other hand, you recognize that Dr. Green is using his position as training and supervising analyst to develop a clique of younger colleagues who will support him.

DISCUSSION

The inevitable transference feelings of the younger colleagues toward Dr. Green make it difficult for them to express their genuine feelings and reactions. Similar to the candidate who informed you of this from the analytic couch, the others of the younger group fear Dr. Green's retaliation if they do not support him and feel uneasy at being pressured by a senior and well-respected individual. Dr. Green appears to be using his transference position for younger colleagues to gratify his own ambitions and personal needs for recognition in the election and as such is not recognizing, or is ignoring, awareness of the considerable pressure that this exerts on the younger colleagues.

The development of such a clique is considered inappropriate in accordance with the Ethics code, but the knowledge that it is occurring is also a difficult burden for you to maintain in regard to the coming election. At the same time, the psychological pressures on the candidates and younger colleagues seem to be damaging to the psychoanalytic community and you feel something should be done to mitigate this pressure.

While not using the confidences of the analysand, it may be possible to alert yourself vis-a-vis other pieces of data to confirm or to refute the behavior of Dr. Green. If alerted by the candidate analysand, you are then in a position to find other evidences away from the couch to the effect of Dr. Green's impact on younger colleagues, it may then be possible to bring this up with a variety of other colleagues and Society officers who may be in a position to share the burden. They may also be in a position to bring to the attention of the current administration of the Society the issue of Dr. Green's electioneering behavior. Hopefully, this would then be referred to the Psychoanalyst Assistance Committee which might then bring to Dr. Green's attention the existence of concern about his behavior and potentially allow the analytic group to emphasize to him the inappropriateness of his actions. Hopefully, this would help avoid any ethics investigation or charge of inappropriate behavior.

RELATIONSHIPS / Personal (D-2-a)

Dr. Marcus, an advanced psychoanalytic candidate, has been in supervision with Dr. Ryder for the past four years. The supervision has been a significant experience for both of them, and both the patient and the candidate have made encouraging and significant progress in their development. Dr. Ryder has been divorced for the past three years and has had a casual dating relationship with a number of different women. Dr. Marcus has never been married but has had several personal male relationships, none of which has been particularly unique or intense.

Both Dr. Marcus and Dr. Ryder find each other extremely compatible, attractive and enjoyable; they seem to share a number of interests as well as the work of the supervisory situation, and each has a significant personal interest in the other.

Following successful termination of the supervised analysis and the cessation of the formal supervisory relationship, Dr. Marcus and Dr. Ryder find themselves together in a variety of social situations involving members of the Psychoanalytic Institute "family," and each develops a further investment in the other. At this point, Dr. Ryder asks Dr. Marcus to attend a concert with him and they have an extremely compatible, pleasant evening, each finding the other to be a "kindred spirit." They agree to begin a regular social dating relationship.

Is this an ethical problem? If so, what are the specific ethical issues that are applicable? If not, how does this new relationship differ from the proscription of personal relationships between analyst and former analysand?

RELATIONSHIPS / Personal (D-2-b)

Dr. Albert and Dr. Zimmer are training and supervising analysts who are on the faculty of a Psychoanalytic Institute. Dr. Albert has in supervision a candidate who is the analysand of Dr. Zimmer. Dr. Albert and Dr. Zimmer have very sharply differing theoretical and clinical views on the nature of the analytic process and on appropriate psychoanalytic technique. The candidate who is being analyzed by Dr. Zimmer is demonstrating in his supervisory work some of the theoretical and clinical ideas that he experienced in his analysis with Dr. Zimmer.

Dr. Albert finds the candidate reluctant and repetitively

unwilling to accept suggestions or recommended changes in his psychoanalytic work with his patient and has become increasingly negative in his perception of the candidate's work. Recently, this led to a significant and contemptuous criticism of Dr. Zimmer as well as of his psychoanalytic theoretical understanding, made directly to the candidate during a supervisory session. The candidate, in the course of his analytic work, described and detailed Dr. Albert's criticisms, feeling very uncomfortable and aware that he, the candidate, was being used to convey a message from Dr. Albert to Dr. Zimmer.

Is this an ethical issue? If so, what are the ethical questions that this situation raises? Is this a problem of pedagogic technique? What options does the candidate have? How can personal issues be separated from professional differences? What are the responsibilities of Dr. Albert and Dr. Zimmer, as well as the institute administration? How might this situation be resolved?

DISCUSSION

Dr. Albert's behavior towards his supervisee is not clearly unethical as much as it is lacking in sensitivity, judgment and educational competency. Certainly, the candidate should not be exposed to a "contemptuous criticism" of his analyst's views. Nor would the candidate profit from an "increasingly negative" view of his work by his supervisor. This leads to a destructive educational environment. Dr. Albert, the supervisor, has two available options. He could tell the candidate that he and Dr. Zimmer have quite different views about theoretical and clinical issues and therefore the supervisory match could lead to an unproductive and even uncomfortable educational experience. A straightforward presentation of the supervisor's dilemma and decision to bow out need not be carried out by saying anything negative about the candidate. Hopefully, the departing supervisor might in an honest way find it possible to find some aspects of the supervisee's work that are praiseworthy.

The other alternative available to Dr. Albert is to continue the supervision in an attempt to be helpful to the supervisee in whatever ways are possible, given the differences between his views and those of Dr. Zimmer. In a respectful way Dr. Albert could present alternative views of theory and technique for the candidate's consideration without directly attacking the candidate's analyst. In an atmosphere of tolerance and patience, candidates may be willing to consider and try out analytic approaches that differ from those of their analyst. In some instances when a candidate is not benefiting personally from analysis, an alternative approach proposed by a supervisor may even be sufficiently convincing to the candidate to eventually lead to changing analysts. This hopefully would arise from the candidate's own deliberations and not be a result of the supervisor's agenda.

The candidate also has options. The candidate could request another supervisor which should be granted without prejudice. It is also possible, although not likely, that the candidate could have a frank discussion with the supervisor that could lead to a more appropriate pedagogic atmosphere. In some cases, it might be appropriate for the candidate both to change supervisors and to lodge a formal complaint about the inappropriate supervisory behavior. Such a complaint might lead to a useful collegial discussion with the supervisor. This could best be accomplished in a confidential setting with no more than two other faculty members appointed by the Education Committee chair or drawn from the membership of either the Ethics or the Psychoanalyst Assistance Committee.

The one course of action that should not be followed by the candidate is to continue this increasingly unprofitable and abusive supervisory relationship without taking some action to change the situation. The candidate must feel that efforts to improve the situation will not be held against him or her and that all complaints and concerns will be taken seriously and acted upon appropriately.

E. Safeguarding The Public And The Profession

The need to protect the public against incompetent or unethical practitioners exists in every profession, but the isolated and confidential nature of psychoanalytic practice makes it difficult to assess an individual's functioning. In addition, the analyst's functioning cannot be judged by therapeutic success or failure in a particular case, since these outcomes are the result of multiple complex variables. The use of consultation is highly recommended as a way to maintain both quality of practice and protection of patients.

When a psychoanalyst becomes concerned about how the treatment is going, and particularly about his or her involvement with a patient, it is advisable to obtain a consultation. The particular issues that most need consultation are those in which countertransference feelings become difficult to handle, or actions that may represent boundary crossings or boundary violations become evident.

A very important aspect of a consultation is the selection of the consultant. It is tempting to select somebody who is comfortable, a good friend, and who will not be seen as likely to be critical. A friend, however, is not likely to be able to be objective. It is important to consult a person who is experienced, but not seen as primarily critical, punitive, or dogmatic. It is extremely important to be able to give the consultant all possible information. Just as in a psychoanalytic treatment, shame or guilt may cause withholding and this will make a successful consultation more difficult, if not impossible. A token consultation from a primarily supportive friend is not going to be genuinely helpful. A good friend may have difficulty being really honest.

Although it is necessary for the consultant to be trusted, an optimal distance is necessary in order to create an atmosphere in which the consultant can really be helpful. Otherwise the danger is that the consultation will not be used effectively, and the problems will not be resolved. Another problem can develop if the consultant has several roles. A therapist, an employer, a colleague who shares a practice, all can have conflicts of interest which may interfere with objectivity.

A very strong identification of the consultant with the analyst can create problems, in that the consultant's self-protectiveness can interfere with fully listening. For a consultation to be effective, the consultant must learn as much of the whole story as possible. If the data are incomplete because the consultant cannot listen, the usefulness of the consult will be severely limited.

The consultant must create an atmosphere of tolerance and acceptance and avoid embarrassing or humiliating the person seeking the consultation. On the other hand, it is equally important to not offer support without at the same time offering the opportunity to fully understand all aspects of the situation. Support in that case can be empty or misleading if it is understood as approval rather than help in understanding and responding appropriately.

Consultations should be a formal arrangement, whether as a single session or a series. Informal, or so-called "corridor discussions," are not true consultations; and while they may serve to reassure the treating analyst, they are not appropriate as a means of assuring professional ethical responsibility. It is essential to obtain enough data about a situation to have the basis for forming an independent opinion.

The principle of safeguarding the profession and the public may place an analyst in a situation of conflict with other ethical principles, or there may be conflict with personal or collegial relationships. Concern for the welfare of friends and colleagues may make this ethical obligation very difficult, but the need to safeguard the public and the profession makes this an area that deserves our utmost efforts.

SAFEGUARDS / ANALYST-INITIATED CONSULTATION (E-1)

Dr. Carter received a call from a colleague Dr. Sutton requesting an urgent consultation. When Dr. Sutton arrived she described the following situation, seeking help from Dr. Carter in understanding what had occurred.

Dr. Sutton had been functioning at her usual level and was enjoying her psychoanalytic practice. Recently, Dr. Sutton found herself having some sexual fantasies about a particular young man who was experiencing an eroticized transference relationship to her. She was aware of his seductiveness, as well as of his past history of having been sexually abused as a child. For the first three years of the analysis the process had unfolded effectively, and there was progressive improvement and change in the patient, his behavior, his symptoms, and his sense of self-esteem. Dr. Sutton felt a sense of professional pride in her work and in the patient's progress, and had not been aware of any major disruptive countertransference impulses or fantasies.

However, a week ago she woke from a sexual dream involving her patient, and she noted in subsequent analytic sessions that she was preoccupied with erotic fantasies. Two days before the consultation, Dr. Sutton embraced the patient as he arose from the couch and kissed him passionately on the lips as he left the hour.

Badly shaken by her own awareness of the inappropriateness of her behavior and countertransference enactment, Dr. Sutton struggled to understand and recognize the disturbance within herself. When the patient returned the following day, Dr. Sutton indicated to him directly that what had occurred the previous day was a response based on her countertransference and that she would need to understand and analyze her behavior; and she hoped it would not disrupt the course of the effective psychoanalytic work that was being done between them.

Dr. Carter listened to the account given by Dr. Sutton and recognized that Dr. Sutton felt extremely guilty and felt that she had betrayed her analytic role. She was ashamed at her failure to maintain the analytic situation with her patient. She seemed not to understand origins or the nature of her counter-transference with this particular patient, since this had been an apparently isolated event in her practice. Dr. Sutton was also clearly asking for help to cope with the situation and therapeutic process.

What options does Dr. Carter have? What are his obligations to the patient and to the profession in regard to Dr. Sutton's countertransference and its enactment? What are his obligations to Dr. Sutton as a colleague asking for help? What can he reasonably expect of the consultation? What is his duty to report inappropriate violations by a colleague in an attempt to maintain responsibility to the profession? Has the analysis conducted by Dr. Sutton been irretrievably compromised? Is this an analyzable boundary crossing?

SAFEGUARDS / PATIENT-INITIATED CONSULTATION (E-2-a)

Mrs. Arnold was a middle-aged woman who entered analysis with Dr. Stevens for symptoms of chronic depression, dissatisfaction with her life experience, marital tension, and the wish to better understand her traumatic background. At the time of her entry into analysis, she was functioning effectively as a legal secretary. She had not been involved in any type of sustained psychotherapy, although she had received counseling from another therapist for short periods of time in connection with specific marital issues. Her decision to enter analysis was the hope for a definitive and sustained therapeutic experience which would allow her to feel more responsive in her marriage, and more fulfilled and satisfied with herself.

Initially the analysis seemed to be going well, and the patient developed a dependent and intensely needful transference relationship to the analyst in which the focus was primarily upon her increasing recognition and awareness of the disappointments that she had experienced in her relationship with her mother as a child. She began to explore previously unrecognized feelings of ambivalence and resentment at her mother's attention to a younger brother and to the sense that the mother had withdrawn her interest in the patient at the time of the birth of the younger brother. The patient began to recover memories and feelings of loneliness, depression, and feeling unworthy and angry towards her mother, along with a sense that her relationship with her father had not significantly protected her nor compensated her for the absence of the maternal nurturance for which she yearned.

After the first year of the analysis, as the awareness of these "maternal deprivations" were increasingly experienced and exposed during the analytic sessions, the patient's behavior began to shift; she became increasingly handicapped, both at work and in her marital relationship by feelings of worthlessness, a sense of hopelessness and feelings of profound depression with some suicidal preoccupation.

The behavior outside the analysis was expressed in a parallel fashion during analytic sessions in which she would appear depressed, deeply distressed and in pain, crying and feeling alone and experiencing a sense of desperation. It was in this context that on one occasion her request for a hug from the analyst at the end of a session was granted and a brief hug intended for reassurance was offered by the analyst.

Subsequently this became a regular part of the analytic encounter, and the patient was hugged and, in return, hugged the analyst after each session as she prepared to leave the office. Occasionally, at the patient's request, the analyst would sit next to the patient on the couch allowing the patient to put her arms around him as they continued to talk about the analytic material and the expression of increasing awareness of the patient's deep yearning for maternal nurturance, care, and the fantasy of making up for past deprivations in this regard.

Throughout this time, the patient's behavior, both inside the analysis and outside in her life at work and with her family, deteriorated further. She became increasingly desperate, depressed, potentially suicidal and demanding of attention and concern from the analyst. The patient experienced long episodes of silence with the analyst attempting to encourage her verbalization but being unsuccessful in doing so. The hugs at the end of the session at the door were continuing regularly.

These behaviors were never subjected to verbal attention, curiosity, or discussion. Eventually she confided in a friend who encouraged the patient to seek consultation and advice from a mental health professional.

In the consultation with Dr. Morton, the patient described her deep and prolonged attachment to her analyst with a variety of intense pre-oedipal fantasies and a description of how important the elements of the physical contact with the analyst progressively became. In her words, the entire session was a prelude to the moments of physical hugging at the end or the times when the analyst would sit on the couch next to her. She felt sexually stimulated at times, but ultimately frustrated.

The consultant advised the patient that her analysis with Dr. Stevens was compromised and that it would be most appropriate to change to another analyst and discontinue her analytic work with Dr. Stevens. The patient reported the recommendation to Dr. Stevens at the next session.

In response to this, Dr. Stevens sought consultation to discuss the events and process with a consultant. For Dr. Stevens, the issue had been an evaluation of the patient as having a personality disorder and whose primary attachment and relationship with her mother had been seriously flawed and disturbed. His intention and therapeutic rationale was the attempt to make meaningful, effective and restorative contact with the patient at a deeply experienced affective level in whatever ways or by whatever techniques were possible. He saw the hugging and the other physical contacts as concrete expressions of concern, attention, and comfort needed by the patient so that she could overcome her primary suspicion and disappointment in all interpersonal relationships. He had not experienced the contact as sexually stimulating and had no awareness of such experience or interpretation by the patient. His aim was primarily to keep his patient from suicide and able to maintain a sense of hope in the potential for analytic understanding. For him the various elements of physical contact represented needed concrete illustrations to the desperately ill patient of analytic concern, support and attempts to reach and maintain a needed nurturance. He expressed his concern at observing the patient's profound deterioration but he hoped that his approach would eventually be effective.

Is this an ethical question or one of psychoanalytic technique? Is this an iatrogenic situation or is the difficulty due primarily to the patient's psychopathology. Should Dr. Stevens have sought consultation earlier? What options exist for the patient, her analyst and the consultant? What is a psychoanalyst's ethical responsibility regarding possible self destructive behavior by a patient?

SAFEGUARDS / Patient-Initiated Consultation (E-2-b)

Robert and Jane Adams are a professional couple living in a large metropolitan area. Jane Adams completes a long and difficult, but ultimately quite successful, analysis with Dr. Wright. In the latter part of the analysis, Robert Adams seems to be suffering from depression about the marriage and relationship with his rejuvenated wife. Nothing is done other than consultations with a psychopharmacologist who prescribes an antidepressant medication. The medication offers some relief of symptoms but Robert remains unhappy about the relationship with Jane even after she terminates her analysis, and he is less available for companionship and comfort

Quite concerned, Jane encourages Robert to see Dr. Wright, whom she regards as a miracle worker, the best that there is in their area. Robert sees Dr. Wright and begins consultations with him. Urged into treatment and then analysis by Jane, Robert is accepted by Dr. Wright as an analysand; he feels he can help him because he knows so much about Jane and the marital situation. As Robert regresses in the analytic process, he becomes less available to Jane which rekindles the original problems for which she sought treatment. She asks to see Dr. Wright after talking with Robert about how much she is suffering.

Dr. Wright decides after seeing Jane that he cannot see both Robert and Jane in analysis and that Robert needs to be analyzed now while Jane can see him intermittently in consultations. The decision does not sit well with Jane and all of the problems become intensified. Finally, she breaks off all of her own consultations with Dr. Wright and also urges Robert to end his work with Dr. Wright. Her estimation of Dr. Wright falls, and she becomes furious at him for his bad judgment and betrayal of her continued needs to be his patient. The marriage becomes more difficult when she finds new treatment through a consultant and in time, brings an ethics action against Dr. Wright. Robert's treatment is in jeopardy and finally becomes impossible. He joins Jane in her complaint against Dr. Wright as he finds a new analyst and recognizes the nature of this impossible situation.

What are the ethical issues in this situation? Does Jane's complaint have merit? Are there issues of technique in Dr. Wright's decisions? Is it ethical for an analyst to use information or be influenced by information from a former analysand in the analysis of a patient closely related to the former analysand? What might Dr. Wright have done to prevent this unfortunate situation? Would there be a difference if this occurred in a small community with limited analytic help available, rather than a large metropolitan area? What are an analyst's obligations toward former analysands?

F. IMPLEMENTATION
OF THE CODE

Implementing the Code of Ethics will be a challenge both to individual analysts and to psychoanalytic institutes and societies. Serious conflicts may be activated, particularly if the involved colleague is a friend or a revered senior analyst. Many factors will be involved including awareness of one's own fallibility, denial of one's own vulnerability, conflicting loyalties and concern for reputations, both personal and professional. Often rumors are spread about and cannot be refuted since the inquiries into ethical violations should be confidential.

The Code of Ethics expects the individual analyst and the analytic group to take action to protect patients, students, the public and the profession when violations are brought to their attention. The usual non-judgmental therapeutic attitude is not appropriate since a position must be taken, an investigation conducted, and possibly action must follow.

There have been many instances where violations have been noted for years and nothing has been done. Not taking action negatively impacts the analytic community since the unethical analyst may continue to damage those under his or her influence. In addition, younger colleagues and students may accept this inaction as normative and identify with it, thus continuing the tradition of tolerance for unethical behaviors.

For institutes or societies, this implementation requirement can be time consuming and financially draining and can produce conflicting loyalties. It may even activate previously dormant issues and conflict within the group and become divisive in a destructive way. Yet it remains an issue for the individual analyst, as well as an institutional responsibility for the administration and the community as a whole.

IMPLEMENTATION OF CODE /
Individual Responsibility (F-1)

Rumors are circulating through a psychoanalytic institute and society to the effect that a particular senior psychoanalyst has been fondling and having sexual relations with some of his female patients. The most detailed and persuasive of these rumors comes from an analysand in your practice who reports the information as part of her psychoanalytic material during analytic sessions. She is deeply distressed by this and wonders if these reports are true and whether or not it implies license for the behavior of analysts in regard to their analysands. You have no direct information or observations of your own in regard to the rumors.

What options do you have and what responsibilities do you have in this situation? What are the likely consequences of whatever option you choose?

DISCUSSION

This situation involves a conflict between ethical principles. The principle of confidentiality for the patient and the patient's material suggests that the analyst may not reveal the information heard from a patient. However, the need to protect the public and the profession requires that psychoanalysts should protect patients, the profession, and the public against any practice of psychoanalysts that demonstrates an absence of professional competence or the compromise of ethical standards. This implies the need for investigation of the colleague, but psychoanalysts should be respectful of their colleagues. In addition, you are unsure how much the patient's strongly positive and erotic transference is a factor in her bringing this material up at this time. You could see if the other sources of information about this behavior are sufficiently convincing to initiate activating the Ethics Committee to look into the rumors. Collective, rather than individual investigation is appropriate. The question of the analysand's motivations in bringing this information to you must be analyzed as part of her treat-

ment. If she is close to one or more of the females who are al-legedly being abused, a good question is why she does not ad-vise them to initiate a complaint. This will certainly make it clear that this behavior, if accurately described, is not consid-ered professionally appropriate.

IMPLEMENTATION OF CODE /
INSTITUTIONAL RESPONSIBILITY (F-2-a)

Rumors are circulating throughout the analytic community in regard to a particular psychoanalyst who is rumored to be abusing and violating the boundaries of patients in a variety of non-sexual ways. The rumors are widespread, and a number of people who have direct supervisory, analysand, or friendship relationships with the analyst in question feel that he is being inappropriately and unfairly picked upon for things that others also do in the conduct of their practices. Another large group in the analytic community feels that this kind of behavior in the analyst in question cannot be tolerated and that it brings disrespect on the profession and presents a very poor model for the current candidates in the training program.

The administration of the Institute has informally talked with the analyst in question, and he has flatly and vociferously denied all of the allegations suggested in the rumors. The analytic community is sharply divided as to whether or not the rumors have substance. The analyst in question has retained legal counsel, and the director of the Institute has received a letter from this lawyer indicating the possibility of a lawsuit for slander and monetary damage if an ethics investigation is conducted and subsequent publicity ensues.

The Institute's financial situation is relatively precarious, and the financing of operations for the educational program is mainly sustained by personal contributions, chiefly from the analytic community itself.

What should the administration of the Institute do? Recognizing the probable expense of a lengthy legal investigation and possible court action, should they proceed with an ethics investigation and process? Recognizing the split in the opinions and feelings of the various members of the analytic community, what can they do to resolve the differences? Should they refer the entire matter to the state licensing commission in the discipline that the analyst represents? Given the possibility that the licensing commission is not familiar with psychoanalytic ethical principles and also that the usual investigation by the state commission involves a lengthy and uncertain time process, can the current situation be allowed to continue? Should they arrange a general analytic community meeting to discuss openly the issues in question?

IMPLEMENTATION OF CODE /
INSTITUTIONAL RESPONSIBILITY (F-2-b)

The psychoanalytic society has received a written complaint from a patient in analysis to the effect that her analyst, Dr. Abadi, has been engaging in sexual relations with her during her sessions. The society president forwards the complaint to the ethics committee and reminds the chairperson that they are a small society with a tight budget. At the same time he requests, according to the society bylaws, that the ethics committee hold a preliminary investigation of the charges.

The committee chairperson notifies Dr. Abadi of the charge and of the name of the individual who is making it and, at the same time, invites him to appear at an informal committee hearing on a specific date. The committee also asks the patient, Mrs. Yates, to appear on a given date separately from Dr. Abadi. The committee meets with Mrs. Yates, who describes the pattern of increasing sexual intimacy leading to sexual intercourse during the patient's analytic hours. At first, she was both frightened and thrilled that the analyst was showing this kind of interest in her, and she participated willingly. As time continued, however, she became increasingly guilt ridden, shamed and felt that the analysis was no longer proceeding in a therapeutic manner. When she tried to raise these issues as part of her therapy with Dr. Abadi, she quotes him as saying that "this is an acceptable part of a treatment experience", inasmuch as she had been extremely frightened and inhibited in regard to her sexuality, which was one of the symptoms that brought her to treatment. In a discussion of the interview after the patient had left, the committee members felt that she was a credible individual, and there was a general consensus that her complaint was valid.

At the appointed time, Dr. Abadi appeared before the ethics committee accompanied by legal counsel. The committee indicated to Dr. Abadi and counsel the gist of Mrs. Yates' complaint and asked Dr. Abadi for his account of the therapy and of the nature of their relationship as it applied to her complaint. Upon advice of counsel, Dr. Abadi declined to say anything and reiterated that he would not, in any way, cooperate with the ethics committee investigation. After several attempts by the committee to point out that this was only a preliminary investigation and that the results of the investigation would remain confidential, Dr. Abadi continued to maintain his silence and refusal to participate in the investigation. The committee had no choice but to excuse Dr. Abadi and counsel and then to discuss what their course of action could be.

What options does the committee have? Recognizing that there will be significant legal expense in pursuing any inquiry or other option and that the budget of the society is unable to sustain large legal fees, what are the responsibilities to the profession and to the protection of patients in general? What are the likely outcomes of various courses of action and what further trauma might the patient suffer? What can and should be done about Dr. Abadi's membership in the society? What are the implications of the concept of due process that impact upon this situation?

IMPLEMENTATION OF CODE /
INSTITUTIONAL RESPONSIBILITY (F-2-c)

Rumors are circulating throughout the psychoanalytic community that Dr. Fowler, a senior and well respected training analyst, has been seriously depressed since he underwent major surgery three years ago. He had returned to full practice after a normal convalescence and was living alone following the death of his wife five years before.

His depression seemed to have lifted significantly in the past year and additional rumors were circulating in the community that this corresponded to the time when he was beginning to be seen in the community in the company of a young female analysand. The analytic community seemed paralyzed and unable to respond effectively to this situation, although there was increasing awareness that something needed to be done.

Finally, the ethics committee chairperson contacted Dr. Fowler and asked that he meet informally with several of the ethics committee members to discuss the rumors and concerns of the analytic community.

Dr. Fowler agreed and acknowledged to the subcommittee that he indeed had thought himself to be deeply in love with his analysand and that he had begun a deep and intimate personal relationship with her. But he became increasingly aware of how inappropriate this was and approximately four months prior to this meeting, he had discontinued this relationship with her and had hoped that she would seek treatment with someone other than himself. He felt remorseful and distressed and recognized his behavior as having been inappropriate and perhaps due to his personal loneliness and difficulty; he had also decided within himself to retire from practice within the next year which would allow time to complete the cases currently in treatment.

The committee members felt that Dr. Fowler was genuinely remorseful and this was an illustration of the concept of "the love sick analyst" whose unfulfilling personal relationships left him or her vulnerable to poor judgment vis a vis countertransference responses to an analysand. They felt that he had a long and distinguished career and that he would be devastated to be publicly rebuked or censured by the ethics committee. They felt that his decision to retire was an appropriate one and that he needed time to complete his continuing cases and that he would be able to do this under regular monitoring and supervision. They also recognized that since his remaining cases were males, it was unlikely that there would be another boundary violation. The committee decided to accept his request that there be no official sanction and that he be allowed to quietly retire, with private arrangements to monitor his work until that time.

What are the ethical issues in regard to Dr. Fowler, the patient and the analytic community? Was the committee decision appropriate? What would be the effect of this delayed decision on the public and on the analytic practitioners and trainees? Who is responsible for arranging care for the former analysand?

IMPLEMENTATION OF CODE / INSTITUTIONAL RESPONSIBILITY (F-2-d)

Dr. Czerny was a senior institute faculty member, training analyst, and a very popular supervisor. Because of his popularity and position as a source of referrals, many people were reluctant to believe the accusations against him and accepted his denials and his blaming patients for having delusions and distortions.

For some years there had been complaints that he had had sexual relationships with female patients. He worked long hours and weekends and it was said that he spent some of that "working" time in sex. One patient had gone for consultation to her internist. When he heard the story he referred her to an analyst, and she saw another one as well. Each one was prepared to file an ethics complaint, but each time the patient backed down from being open and identified, although it was by then widely rumored in the community. A previous patient had settled a malpractice complaint out of court.

One faculty member brought this issue up in the committee on the impaired psychoanalyst. At first, the committee believed that they could do nothing because no patient had come forward. Then one member filed a complaint with the Institute administration which did mobilize an ethics hearing.

Despite the anxiety at proceeding, a meeting of training analysts was called. After heated discussion, spanning several meetings, Dr. Czerny was removed from his training analyst status. There was controversy about doing this. However, there was a legal opinion that training analyst status was a privilege, not a right. In addition, over the past few months several analysts had been consultants to the patient who was complaining, and so there was first-hand patient information. Meanwhile, the patient did come forward herself and file a complaint.

A number of training analysts voted to renew Dr. Czerny's appointment in spite of this information. A number of factors contributed to the institutional resistance. Denial and reluctance to identify oneself with such behavior in a fellow analyst, fear that publicity will hurt the institution and the hope that the situation could be successfully hidden, all played a role. Rationalizations about not harming patients and blurring the distinctions between an affair and a violation in treatment were also factors. There seemed to be in some analysts a narcissistic over-valuing of their prerogatives and position which contributed to their tolerance of exploitative behaviors.

What are some of the problems in implementing the Code of Ethics in cases of flagrant boundary violations? What are the ethical issues for the individual analyst? What are the ethical issues for the analytic society and institute? In what other ways could this situation be resolved? At what point should licensing authorities be notified of the situation?

G. ETHICAL VIOLATIONS VERSUS TECHNICAL VARIATIONS

Recent developments in the theory and technique of psychoanalysis have significantly expanded our concepts of appropriate therapeutic interactions and processes. In addition, the widening scope of psychoanalysis in reaching increasingly troubled individuals has required alterations in previously standardized proper technique. There has been a progressive change in the culture of the profession in that there are many theoretical differences concerning the definition of appropriate interactions.

Within the Ethics Code there are relatively few moral or ethical absolutes and many of the criteria and issues involve subtleties, differences of theoretical understanding and conceptual variations in regard to the analyst's role. It is possible to have multiple interpretations or rationalizations for most activities or attitudes. In this climate it is highly problematic to make ethical judgments, let alone decisions that must be implemented by actions. Attitudes, behaviors and interactions which might have been seen as violations of proper technique many years ago may, in today's theoretical pluralism, be viewed as acceptable.

There are additional considerations that are unique to psychoanalysis. It must be recognized that there are times when differences in theory and technical approach may be used to rationalize behavior that violates the ethical principles which are expressed in the code. Separating out these various factors will be a challenge to the individual analyst as well as to the analytic community. The private nature of the interaction makes it difficult to objectify questionable behavior, while the transference and countertransference reactions may make objective reporting of possible ethical violations rather unlikely. The use of secondary sources of information makes it even more difficult to objectify complaints.

Finally, the degree and repetitiveness with which an ethical principle has been violated makes evaluation on an objective scale more problematic. For example, those who espouse the therapeutic usefulness of transference-countertransference enactments will interpret them differently than those analysts who believe otherwise.

The distinction between an ethical violation and a technical variation can be an exceedingly difficult task but that does not justify avoidance.

ETHICAL VERSUS TECHNICAL / Therapeutic (G-1-a)

Dr. Turner is treating two patients who were sent from different sources and have different names. As the analytic processes continue he begins to realize that the two patients are related. Neither one knows that he is seeing the other. He hears information about each of them from the other in the course of associations and he is beginning to have difficulty to separating out in his mind what information about each patient comes from which source. Did he learn something directly from the patient, or did it come from the other source?

Should he inform the patients that he is seeing both of them, and that he would not have done this knowing their relationship? Perhaps one of them should be sent to another analyst? Or should he keep quiet about this and just struggle with the difficulty of keeping them separated in his mind? Is this an ethical or a technical question, or both?

ETHICAL VERSUS TECHNICAL / Therapeutic (G-1-b)

Dr. Osman has in analysis a forty-six year old business man whose analytic progress has been substantial and who has been a dedicated and conscientious patient. From the beginning of their analytic agreement, the patient has acknowledged that Dr. Osman will charge for missed appointments and has accepted this as appropriate since he, from time to time, must make out-of-town business trips.

In the third year of his analysis, the patient, without prior history of heart problems, develops over a weekend, a serious myocardial infarction that requires hospitalization and treatment in the ICU. Dr. Osman visits the patient briefly and learns that his heart attack has been a major one, that he needs by-pass surgery, and that it will be several months before the analysand is able to return to normal activity.

What should Dr. Osman do about the five open analytic hours until his patient can return? Should he charge them to the patient? He needs the money to maintain his income level, but should he forgo the charge and suffer the loss? Should he take on another analytic patient using the hours vacated by the analysand who is sick? Should he use that extra open time for other clinical activities? Should he notify the patient that his analytic time will be forfeited because of his illness, and that when he is able to resume analysis, he can do so when and if Dr. Osman will have the time? Is this primarily an ethical question or is it a question of psychoanalytic technique?

ETHICAL VERSUS TECHNICAL / Therapeutic (G-1-c)

Dr. Mehta awakens one morning with a heavy cough, chills, fever and general muscle achiness. He calls his physician who diagnoses the flu and prescribes medication for symptomatic relief, encouraging Dr. Mehta to stay in bed for at least the duration of his symptoms. Dr. Mehta is a conscientious and dedicated analyst with a deep commitment to his work and he calls his patients to cancel their sessions for the next three days explaining that he has "the flu".

After three days, the symptoms have abated somewhat but Dr. Mehta still feels weak, preoccupied with his difficulty and still has a significant cough although the acute phase of his illness has subsided.

Dr. Mehta is torn by the conflicts between his own physical illness and needs for rest and the expectations and needs of his patients, particularly those who are involved in deep transference relationships where fears of abandonment and separation have been particularly prominent. He is aware that his illness is not fully resolved and that his own capacity for optimal energy and concentration are probably still restricted. Yet at the same time, he feels an obligation to return to practice as soon as feasible, particularly since several of his patients are specifically vulnerable to interruptions of relationships.

Is this an ethical issue? Is this an issue relating to analytic technique? What is the optimal balance between the needs of the analyst and the responsibility to the patient? What would you do in such a situation?

DISCUSSION

Dr. Mehta should be praised for canceling his appointments when he was initially ill. Although we often observe analysts who practice while ill, this is not in the best interest of patients and sets a poor example of self care. The capacity to look after oneself when ill is an important part of normal behavior. It is not good practice to work when affected by acute symptoms that interfere with performance. Also in the acute phase of a flu-like illness the analyst exposes the patient to contagion.

Sometimes when analysts continue working while ill, they may believe that they are motivated by concern for patients, but the reality may be that the motivation is financial gain or guilt about cancelling. Other needs of the analyst may include the need to deny any weakness or the passivity of being ill. There is also the fantasy of narcissistic invulnerability as well as the self-satisfying portrait of the analyst as the sacrificing and indispensable caretaker.

When Dr. Mehta resumes practice after the acute phase of illness, we can assume that the motivation is the welfare of his vulnerable patients. Perhaps he could return selectively to part-time practice with these patients and use the remaining time to fully recover from his illness. He would have to balance the non- neurotic concern for his complete recovery with the best interests of his patients. The solution for each analyst and each situation might be very varied according to the factors involved. In the recovery phase of an acute illness, there is no one answer that fits all situations.

ETHICAL VERSUS TECHNICAL / THERAPEUTIC (G-1-d)

Drs. James and Rita Hobson are a well known psychoanalytic couple who live in a large, psychoanalytically dense metropolitan area. If James were an attorney with a large law firm, he would be called a "rainmaker," a partner who has the capacity to bring in business to the firm.

An analyst of considerable charm and wit, James attracted people and enjoyed the reputation of a busy and competent analyst with a full practice. His wife Rita, more ordinary by all of these standards, was herself hard working and competent. James encouraged colleagues to refer to Rita, and he also referred spouses of some of his patients to her. Sometimes he found a way of telling his patients that Rita was very good at working with the particular problems under discussion.

James found ways of seeing to it that Rita was aware of his needs for referrals also and made it clear that he could see her patients in complex work, as well as doing short-term problem solving with some of her patients and their families.

This pattern of practice led to difficulty when the spouse of a patient of his, Betty, was referred to Rita. The referral not only didn't work out, but it became indirectly difficult for Betty's husband, who felt deceived by James, left treatment and brought a complaint to the ethics committee of their institute.

What are the ethical issues involved when one spouse regularly refers patients to the other spouse? What are some of the transference and countertransference factors that may be intensified? Is there an inherent conflict of interests in such a practice?

ETHICAL VERSUS TECHNICAL / THERAPEUTIC (G-1-e)

Dr. Bayer has in analysis an extremely attractive and talented young woman for whom the chief difficulty has been the failure of relationships with men and her sense of being unacceptable and rejected by them. During the first two years of the analysis the patient cautiously and slowly expressed positive feelings and attachments for Dr. Bayer, including some relatively restricted sexual fantasies about him.

Over a time span of several months, Dr. Bayer found himself increasingly attracted by the analysand and began to make comments during the analytic sessions about how attractive she was. Consciously he was trying to enhance her self-esteem. The patient initially felt both surprised and pleased that he found her attractive.

As the analytic process proceeded further, Dr. Bayer made a variety of direct observations about the patient's appearance, attractiveness, and the beauty of her body and legs and described in detail how a man might make love to her given the opportunity. She was particularly stimulated when he confided that he had had a frankly sexual dream with orgasm about her.

At no time did he make any physical overtures, and with respect to the time of sessions, fee and other arrangements of the analytic process, he maintained scrupulous boundaries.

In her associations, the patient complained that while she was stimulated by the things Dr. Bayer was saying, the situation was hopeless because of their professional relationship, and she felt sexually teased and frustrated by his verbal comments. Dr. Bayer responded that he was trying to demonstrate the possibilities of an appropriate male relationship and to help her improve her sense of femininity and sexual appeal. But the patient said that whenever she tried to discuss her actual relationships with men she dated, he seemed to disparage them and to discourage further efforts to date.

Is this an ethical or a technical issue? Does the verbal sexual interaction represent a sexual boundary violation? Does the fact that no physical contact between analyst and patient occurred change the situation?

ETHICAL VERSUS TECHNICAL / THERAPEUTIC (G-1-f)

A 51-year-old man who had just lost his mother was trying to arrange for a surrogate to bear a child for him. Because these arrangements were illegal where he lived, he had to go to another state to accomplish this purpose. He was focused on his goal and going to accomplish it no matter what the cost. He had also just broken an engagement of many years, because he discovered that his fiancée was post menopausal and therefore unable to bear his child. He had no qualms about his desires and was involved with the practical arrangements which were quite complex.

The analyst was actively interpreting and trying to get him to reconsider his actions in view of his total psychodynamic situation. He agreed with the interpretations about his losses but proceeded with his intentions. He had no doubts about his intentions. It was the analyst who was concerned about his desire to arrange for a child to raise. The analyst was concerned for the future both of his patient and for the prospective child.

Is this a proper ethical concern or is it mainly a technical issue? What are the analyst's responsibilities for the results of an analysand's behavior? What are the analyst's options in this situation?

ETHICAL VERSUS TECHNICAL / THERAPEUTIC (G-1-g)

Dr. Ryan has been planning for six months for his wife and himself to attend his 50th college reunion. It will be a week-long celebration involving both academic and intellectually stimulating discussions, as well as various social events and activities, and a number of his college friends have already indicated their intention to attend. He has in analysis a 47-year-old woman whose father died unexpectedly when she was an early adolescent, and they have spent much time discussing her sense of the unexpected abandonment by people whom she counts on as contributing to her chronic difficulties in interpersonal relationships. Dr. Ryan has told his analysand several weeks in advance that he will be out of the city for the week of the reunion, and they have already been discussing the feeling of disappointment that she will have to miss her sessions.

One week before the cancellation is to begin, the patient's husband has a massive heart attack, is hospitalized in the I.C.U. and dies within about six hours. She calls Dr. Ryan on the phone to inform him of the situation; he is fully aware of how devastated she is and how difficult this reenactment of her adolescent trauma will be for her. She also voices some suicidal concerns and the wish to join her husband since she feels she cannot carry on without him.

What should Dr. Ryan do? His absence will undoubtedly exacerbate his analysand's distress and sense of having been abandoned and may well undo some of the trust established over the previous two years of analytic work. He is aware that even in normal times, his summer vacations have been the stimulus for enormous feelings of abandonment and helplessness for this analysand. He and his wife have been looking forward to the reunion and discussing it with friends for a number of months, and it will be the only opportunity that he has to reunite with some of his old friends. He has an office mate who could cover for him and supply immediate care to the analysand.

Whose interests should prevail? What would be the effect if he were to carry out his plans to attend the reunion? What would be the effects on the subsequent analysis if he were to cancel his plans for the reunion and instead remain to care for her during her acute reaction to the death of her husband? Is this an ethical issue? Is this a technical issue? What would you do?

ETHICAL VERSUS TECHNICAL / THERAPEUTIC (G-1-h)

An analyst nods off to sleep momentarily towards the end of a seemingly uneventful hour in the fourth month of an analysis that has been going well. He awakens to hear the patient say, "I guess I've run out of things to say for today. Our time's about up anyway." This was not a usual way for the patient to end an hour. Looking at the clock, the analyst realizes that the most he could have nodded off was one minute or even less. He is not sure whether the patient sensed his absence, but he felt that the hour ended awkwardly.

During the next hour the patient does not mention the ending of the last hour until asked about it and then says "I just ran out of things to say. I don't know that there's anything more to say about it." Later on he does admit that something odd did occur at the end of the previous session and says "It felt odd, as if you weren't present or possibly even asleep." As the analyst tries to explore perceptions and fantasies, the patient asks directly, "Well, were you asleep?" The analyst inquires again about what lies behind the question and the patient associates for a while but asks again, "Well, were you asleep?" Should the analyst admit that he did nod off? Should he apologize?

Does it make any difference if the analyst is unsure about whether he was having a countertransference reaction or was overly tired from a late night?

DISCUSSION

It seems clear that an enactment occurred and eventually must be addressed. Although the patient asks a direct question in the next session, the analyst's first response should be clinical and concern the affects and fantasies that lie behind the question. Was the patient experiencing that the analyst was not interested in anything else that he had to say for that day? Was there an aggressive component in the form of a fantasy that he had somehow silenced the analyst, or had done nothing to keep him awake and alive? Was the patient trying to deny the analyst's mistake by ending the hour himself? A direct answer and apology could cut short the process of looking at the interaction analytically and an opportunity to explore the transference would be missed. But although the analyst should hold off from answering directly, it should be done in a way that emphasizes the analytic value at looking at what occurred. The patient's ability to ask such a question directly should be acknowledged in terms of the progress of the analysis.

But besides the clinical importance of the encounter, there is also an ethical dimension that cannot be ignored. The treatment relationship is founded upon truthfulness. But truthfulness does not have to be so literally interpreted that an immediate answer is required, because that could undermine the analyst's obligation to use his best efforts to foster the analytic process for the benefit of the patient. Holding off on telling the truth could be justified for compelling clinical reasons. This assumes that the patient has been well briefed on the process of psychoanalysis from the beginning of the treatment.

The analyst, however, is expected to treat the patient with respect, and although nothing in the ethics code would require an immediate answer to the patient's question and an apology for the enactment, serious consideration should be given to providing the answer and the apology that this situation would demand in another context. An admission of falling asleep and an apology would show respect for, and validate the accuracy of, the observations of the patient. The psychoanalyst was unavailable for part of the time for which the patient was paying, and this is not fair and competent professional service. Ethically, an admission of shortcoming and an apology would be appropriate and might even have some clinical value for the relationship. It would be difficult to justify deciding never to deal with the reality aspects of the situation, when the clinical exploration has been exhausted and the transference implications have been thoroughly explored.

ETHICAL VERSUS TECHNICAL / INSTITUTIONAL (G-2)

An analysand confides that a friend had told him about the behavior of a faculty member from the same institute as the analyst. He indicated that the faculty member in question, while conducting group supervision in an official institute-sponsored program, would regularly bring a bottle of wine to the session and drink it. He added that during class teaching sessions, this same individual would drink a bottle of wine by himself while teaching and would openly flaunt the behavior in front of the class. The analysand's friend indicated that in both situations the students were distressed and shocked by the behavior, but none felt comfortable in making a public complaint.

The individual analyst is in an ethical dilemma of conflicting principles. There is the principle of confidentiality in regard to the analyst's treatment of his patient. This is opposed to the analyst's need to maintain standards of teaching in the institute, as well as the need to protect the profession by reporting professionally inappropriate and boundary-violating behavior.

The reported behavior may also indicate a substance abuse problem in the colleague in question. This problem would ordinarily require some intervention so that help may be obtained. It would be potentially damaging to the colleague to ignore this need for help, even if he or she is in complete denial.

How can these conflicts be resolved? What are the possible results of various courses of action?

IV. CROSS REFERENCE OF VIGNETTES TO CASE BOOK TABLE OF CONTENTS

110

VIGNETTE PAGE NO..	PRIMARY ISSUES
Page 53	C 2a
Page 54	C 2a
Page 55	C 2b
Page 56	C 2c
Page 57	C 2d
Page 58	C 2d
Page 59	C 2e
Page 60	C 2e,f
Page 61	C 2f,g
Page 64	C 2g
Page 66	C 2g
Page 67	D 1
Page 68	D 1 b
Page 70	D 1c,d
Page 71	D 1d,e
Page 72	D 1f
Page 74	D 1g
Page 75	D 1h
Page 78	D 1i
Page 79	D 2a
Page 80	D 2b
Page 85	E 1
Page 86	E 2a
Page 89	E 2b
Page 92	F 1
Page 93	F 2a
Page 94	F 2b
Page 95	F 2c
Page 97	F 2d
Page 100	G 1a,b
Page 101	G 1c
Page 103	G 1d,e
Page 104	G 1f
Page 105	G 1g
Page 106	G 1h
Page 108	G 2

NOTES

NOTES

NOTES

NOTES

NOTES

NOTES